THE NEGOTIATOR
By L.M. Lacee

Ethics on a Galactic Scale

Copyright
Daughter of Ethos

The NEGOTIATOR Book 1
By L.M. Lacee
Copyright © 2022 L.M. Lacee.

All rights reserved. Published by PrivotelConcepts

CONTENT

THE NEGOTIATOR

Copyright

ONE:

TWO:

THREE:

FOUR:

FIVE:

SIX:

SEVEN:

EIGHT:

NINE:

TEN:

ELEVEN:

TWELVE:

THIRTEEN:

FOURTEEN:

FIFTEEN:

SIXTEEN:

SEVENTEEN:

EIGHTEEN:

NINETEEN:

TWENTY:

TWENTY-ONE:

TWENTY-TWO:

TWENTY-THREE:

TWENTY-FOUR:

TWENTY-FIVE:

TWENTY-SIX:

TWENTY-SEVEN:

TWENTY-EIGHT:
TWENTY-NINE:
THIRTY:
THIRTY- ONE:
THIRTY-TWO:
THIRTY-THREE:
THIRTY- FOUR:
THIRTY-FIVE:
THIRTY-SIX:
THIRTY-SEVEN:
THIRTY- EIGHT:
THIRTY-NINE:
FORTY:
FORTY-ONE:
FORTY-TWO:
FORTY-THREE:
FORTY- FOUR:
FORTY-FIVE:
EPILOGUE:
TRANSLATIONS:

ONE:

Relic Wallace watched the Scout Commander, Matt Karto, say goodnight to his friends and slip through the crowded bar. She had hoped to pluck up the nerve to introduce herself to him tonight. Which is why she had insisted on drinking here and not at home, as she and Echo normally did. But when he made for the door, she saw she had waited too long… again.

Leaning on the bar, Echo said as she too watched the Commander, 'Why don't you talk to him instead of staring after him and drooling into your beer?'

'Shut up.'

'No, I mean it, Relic. He is never going to know you if you won't talk to him.'

'Shut up.'

Echo grinned as she sipped her drink and watched the tall Commander place his hand on the door, then hesitate and swing around to scan the crowd. Instantly, Relic dropped her eyes from the male. Echo stated, 'As your sister, I think I have the right to tell you, you are being an ass about this. It's been what, three going on four luneras since you first started panting after him.'

Relic murmured, 'As your sister, it is my right to shut you up if you don't shut the hayda up right now!' Matt left and Relic breathed easier, then stared at her unrepentant sister and demanded. 'Why do you do that?'

'Because you are an idiot and I am tired of being a sister to an idiot.'

'You know—'

'You are to report to Amahka Elite Kardan's office at 07:00.'

The sisters turned together to stare up at the Warrior who had interrupted their argument. Relic asked, 'Why?'

With a cocky smile, she was sure he had practiced. The

Warrior shrugged, saying. 'No idea, not my department.' With a sketchy salute, he turned and was swallowed up by the crowd.

Relic turned molten eyes on her sister. 'What have you done?'

Echo gasped as she said, 'I've done nothing. Who have you maimed or killed lately?'

Relic ran through the last three or four days and then shook her head. 'No one.'

Echo exclaimed, 'Oh my stars, you had to think about that?'

'Ahh yeah, and shut up.'

'That is … no, I'm at a loss for words.'

'That will be a first.' Downing the rest of her drink, Relic slammed her glass down on the bar. 'I am going to bed. I refuse to be late for a meeting with Kardan.'

Echo agreed. 'Me too. He is handsome but scary.'

'That's true.'

Echo left her half-finished drink, then moved with Relic through the crowd of people who automatically parted for them as they made their way to the exit.

TWO:

Five minutes to seven the following morning found both sisters standing in the corridor outside Kardan's office. 'We are early.' murmured Echo, who then yawned.

'Never too early to make a good impression,' Relic murmured back, smothering a yawn of her own.

'You and your good impressions.'

Relic raised her eyes to her sister as she said, 'Manners are the backbone of a civilized society.'

Echo yawned widely then asked, 'Did you read that?'

'Reading does not kill you. You could stand to pick a book up every now and again.'

'Vids give me everything I need.'

'Death and destruction.'

Echo agreed with a smile. 'If it's done right.'

Annoyed, Relic hissed. 'Stand up straight, walls are not for slouching against.'

Grinning, Echo slouched more and snarled, 'Dearle stars, when did you become such a prissy nag?'

Relic pushed her, forcing her off balance, and snarled, 'Shut up.'

Echo pushed her back and snarled in return, 'You, shut up.'

'Dearle stars, it's like listening to you and one or all of your sisters, without the violence,' Wolf said as he and Peyton walked from her office.

Peyton grinned and said, 'Shut up.'

'No, you shut up.'

'See? It's not just us,' Echo hissed as she and Relic greeted Peyton and Wolf. 'Greetings.'

'Greetings.' replied Peyton. She introduced Wolf to the sisters. 'Allow me to introduce you to sisters with the coolest names.

Echo and Relic Wallace.'

Echo grinned. Every time Peyton introduced her and Relic, she said the same thing. It was amusing, or at least she thought it was. Relic did not, but then Relic was a prissy snob, as Echo often reminded her. Wolf eyed the sisters and asked, 'Why?'

Echo replied with, 'Why what?'

Wolf smiled, 'Why Echo and Relic?'

'Weird assed mother.'

'Oh, I see.'

Relic growled. 'No, she was not weird.' She gave Echo her most disapproving look which she ignored as she ignored all of Relic's disproving expressions. With a smile for Wolf, Relic explained, 'Mother gave me the name Relic because when she gave birth to me, she was looking for artifacts from the past. When Echo was born, her first cries filled the cave mother was in.'

Wolf nodded. 'Interesting.'

Echo muttered. 'Or just plain weird.'

Peyton grinned and asked, 'Are you waiting to see Kardan?'

Relic replied, 'Yes, he asked to see us.'

'Oh, it must be about those rumors.'

'What rumors?'

Peyton smiled vaguely at the three people and waved her hand around. 'Never mind, you will find out soon enough.'

THREE:

Peyton opened the door to Kardan's office and announced, 'I am here and so are Echo and Relic. Why were we waiting in the hall?'

Kardan raised his eyebrows as he stood and replied, 'Because I did not know you were here.'

Peyton nodded. 'This is why you need a full-time assistant like Penny.'

'No, it explains why I did not know you were here, not that I need an assistant.'

'Which you do.'

'Perhaps,' he conceded with a smile.

'Did you forget I was here as well?' Wolf asked Peyton, who turned remorseful eyes on him. He accused her, 'Oh stars, you did. How could you? I just walked with you from your office.'

Peyton felt guilty because she had actually forgotten Wolf was with her. Defensively, she snarled, 'Look here brother, I was —'

Wolf waved his hand, cutting her off and leaving her mouth hanging open as he grumbled in return. 'Yeah… yeah, heard it all before.'

Peyton sniffed dramatically and mumbled, 'So rude!'

Kardan looked past his mate and brother to see Echo and Relic hovering in the doorway. 'Ladies, if you would like to join us, please.'

The sisters nodded in unison and entered the office. It was rumored that when Kardan first arrived on Maikonia, he'd taken over a small office, reportedly no bigger than a cloakroom. Brenda had taken one look at the room and declared the office was not right for the mate of the Star Daughter. Within hours, Kardan found himself surrounded by an office that screamed

Amahka Elite. Relic surreptitiously stared around her at the elegantly masculine room and thought Brenda had got it right: this room suited Kardan, as did the enormous desk he stood behind.

Echo spied Bendrix, Netta's mate and her boss or mentor depending on who you asked, leaning against the far wall. Casually, she walked over and stood next to him. Under the cover of Peyton talking to Kardan, she asked, 'So, do you know why we are here?'

'You have a mission.'

Echo raised her eyebrows at the news, then a smiled crept over her face, causing the normal wariness that lived in her eyes to be replaced with suppressed excitement. After they had settled on Maikonia, both sisters had gone into intensive training. It had horrified Relic to learn Kardan was her direct boss. This had caused her a few sleepless nights until she realized that meant she only reported to him. She told Echo she was relieved to find Hawk and Reeve were responsible for her day-to-day training.

Echo, technically, wasn't an Ambassador (because she wasn't an Ambassador), but she had to go somewhere so Peyton attached her to Bendrix's department. Now she was the proud owner of an office she scarcely spent any time in and was mentored by Bendrix. She had spent the last three luneras training in diplomacy, learning what acceptable and unacceptable behavior was for diplomats and rulers. This usually depended on Peyton and Kardan. If they suspected inappropriate behavior by a world ruler, then she would be sent to deal with said ruler or rulers. She was called a Negotiator, because her job comprised of negotiating a solution to whatever problem the rulers were having or whatever Peyton and Kardan didn't like. After several hours of discussion, Command had rejected her proposal for changing her name to hitman or hitwoman. Her job, she was told, was not to assassinate people. They had Assaens for that. But in saying that, it was up to her to put the world to rights by any means at her disposal.

Under Peyton's guidelines, she could arrange education for the rulers or she could remove the rulers and install someone else or a government to oversee the recommended changes. If either of those options were impossible to accomplish, then she was to find an alternative solution. And killing everyone who annoyed her was not acceptable behavior for the Star Daughter's Negotiator.

She, Bendrix and Domard Jerthem had spent many hours discussing this course of action, usually ending with her storming from the room and then beating a droid to death. Ultimately, it came down to she was there, and they weren't. So, she was to use her best judgment and realize that at the end of the day, she had to live with her decisions, whatever they may be, and now she was to be sent out on her first mission.

Surprised, Echo asked, 'A mission already, really!?'

Bendrix lazily asked, 'Why would I lie?'

Echo scoffed. 'Really? You would lie if it suited you to.'

'I resent that. I lie if I have to, not if it only suits me.'

Echo snorted, 'See what I mean.'

'No,' he turned and faced her, leaning a shoulder against the wall. 'I do whatever I have to, to protect my Suula and our homeworld. If that means doing what you call lying, then so be it.'

Echo unconsciously mimicked his stance as she asked, 'You really don't see lying as terrans do?'

'No, not in the same context as you mean.'

'But surely, if what you promise is a lie—'

He held his hand up, stopping her in mid-sentence. 'To promise something and not deliver is not a lie. It is breaking trust. I never promise anything without knowing I can deliver on my promise.' He shrugged as he turned back to the room. 'The rest is just noise.'

Echo frowned. 'I don't think I understand that logic.'

Bendrix smiled at her confusion. 'See, that is where you are at fault.'

Smiling, herself now, she asked. 'Why?'

'You assume it is logical.'

Echo's exclamation attracted everyone's attention, 'Oh, my stars!'

Peyton smiled sweetly as she politely said, 'I'm sorry, Echo and Ben, please don't let us interrupt your conversation. It's not like this mission is time sensitive or anything.'

Echo asked, 'Are you sure you've finished nagging your mate?'

'You know, I am the Star Daughter.'

'Are you like… bragging now?'

Peyton muttered, 'So rude.'

Relic hurriedly asked Kardan, who was grinning, 'So what is the mission?'

Echo frowned as she looked at her sister. 'What is your problem?'

Relic snapped, 'Sister, just shut up.'

Echo grinned, 'Oh, you and your manners.'

'Seriously?' Relic moaned as she turned pleading eyes on Kardan. 'Are you sure you need her?'

Kardan smiled in response to Relic's plea. 'Yes, you are both immensely qualified for this mission.'

Defeated, Relic asked, 'So what is the mission?'

He picked up two tablets and passed them to the sisters as he said, 'Everything you need to know is in here. You better hurry, your ship leaves in an hour, you will need to pack.'

Echo asked him as she looked over the tablet, 'Staff?'

'Bendrix and Marlo have seen to that.'

'Thank you.' With a formal bow, she said. 'With your permission, Madam Peyton.'

'Granted. And ladies, take care and come home.'

Relic smiled as she tapped her forehead in a salute. 'We will endeavor to do so, Madam.'

FOUR:

Matt stood behind the pillar, waiting for the signal to advance into the dwelling. Impatience gnawed at him like a dog with a bone. Just as he decided this had been a bust, his comm unit tucked inside his ear came to life.

Po' announced, 'We have movement, the window to the left.'

Instantly, every member of his unit's eyes found and locked on the window. This mission was to rescue the family of a government minister who was overseeing the negotiations between two companies for the rights to mine the planet's resources.

The members of Matt's unit for this mission were Po', Ranarra, and Virin, who he had discovered was a resourceful field operative. Not only did he handle the comms and tech for the Scouts, he was a skilled Warrior. He had been on Matt's team for just over three luneras and when Po' left to take up his new assignment, Virin would step into Ranarra's place on the team, leaving Ranarra to take Len's place, when Len took over Po's position.

Matt sighed. He hated the idea of losing Po' but knew his friend was pleased to be considered for the new Commander of a unit assigned to protecting Jean when she began her journey to teach technology to worlds that desperately needed her help. It was a great opportunity for Po' to step out on his own, even so Matt would miss his humor and cussing. 'Is it him?'

'Looks that way.'

Matt softly growled, 'Confirm before we move.'

Po' warned, 'Wait... wait, there is someone with him—'

Impatiently, Matt silently snarled, *hurry the hayda up Po'*.

'No, false alarm. It was a bot.'

'I swear one of these days, Po'.'

Po' laughed as he said, 'Yeah… yeah!'

Virin's voice came over the comm. 'Confirming target is alone now.' Matt counted down the seconds waiting for the all clear. Finally, Virin said, 'It is a go.'

Minutes later, they had rescued the family and killed the pretend kidnappers. Sedeen and Harm held timers and were both grinning when Matt and his unit exited the training building.

Harm praised them. 'You did well. Mission completed under thirty mins. Good work.'

Matt smiled as Sedeen slapped him on his back. 'So, drinks are on you tonight?'

Matt eyed his friend. 'When is it never drinks on me?'

'When it's on Harm.'

Harm gave his brother a dirty look and told Matt and his people, 'Don't forget to see the healers for your check-ups. Sedeen will be buying later for anyone who wants to come.'

Hoots of laughter accompanied this from everyone who had taken part in the exercise. Especially when Sedeen scowled at his brother who told him, 'Do not be so free with other people's credits in the future.'

Sedeen grumbled, 'Are you really my brother?'

'Yes, unfortunately, I have proof.'

'So wrong brother, so wrong!'

Matt left them to their brotherly bickering as he made his way to medical for the after-exercise health check. He met Heather in the hallway. 'Greetings Heather. How are you this day?'

She smiled as she rubbed her slight bulge. 'Greetings Matt. I and my little one are doing just fine, and you?'

'The same as always.'

'And yet, you are here.'

Matt grinned. 'I am on my way for the after-training health check.'

Heather waved him inside her office, 'Come in here and I will do it.' Matt followed her inside. She smiled as she said, 'We have hardly spoken since we returned from the Capital.'

'I know. I have been busy training new scouts. I hear from Harm you have been just as busy. Training all your new recruits, and with the females from Earth, there has not been much time to… how do you say… get together?'

'True.' She tipped her head to the side as she studied him. 'You should come to dinner soon, so we can catch up.'

'I would like that.'

'Sit here, please.' She patted the examination table as she reached for a scanner from the shelf next to the bed.

Matt looked around as he sat on the examination bed. He appreciated Heather's style. The understated colors of browns, greens and gold, with the slight accent of red, fit her well. Practical with a sweet undertone of whimsy, which was a word he had found several nights ago when he was reading a human fairy tale. 'I like your office.'

'Thank you, it suits me.'

'That is what I thought.'

'Have you finished decorating your place?'

Matt sighed. 'Yes, but now I do not think it is right.'

Heather ran the scanner over him as she asked, 'Why? What is wrong with it?'

Matt smiled. 'Nothing, it is just I am not sure my mate will like what I have done.'

Heather stopped mid-scan and stepped back so she could see him better. 'Matt Karto, have you found your mate?'

He nodded shyly. 'I have.' When she went to speak, he hurriedly stated. 'At least I know she is here or was.'

Heather sat on a chair as she asked, 'What does that mean?'

Matt rubbed the back of his neck, a sure sign he was agitated. This is what he had missed lately, talking to Heather about things that mattered. She never talked out of turn, which meant she would not gossip to her sisters. Even if she wanted to, she would not betray his confidence, and she was a great listener. He counted her and Harm among his closest friends.

'I have been catching hints of her for the last few wekens. But

I have not been able to pinpoint who she is, and now she is no longer on world.'

Heather frowned. 'So either she doesn't know about you or she is playing hard to get.'

'Or,' Matt said, 'she is shy.'

Heather tapped her lips with the scanner as she thought about that. 'I suppose that is possible.'

Matt mumbled. 'In the sex classes, they say some females can be extremely shy and a male must have patience.'

'That is true, but now you say she has left Maikonia.'

'Yes.'

'So, is she Terran?'

Matt pulled on his bottom lip for a moment before saying, 'I believe she is.'

'Or,' Heather smiled at him, 'you are hoping she is, and that is why you have not actively sought her out, just in case she is not.'

Matt sighed, 'Perhaps that is so. I find your species so accepting.'

'What has that to do with mating?'

'I fear no other race will accept me as easily for who I am.'

'But Terran females will.'

He nodded. 'You and Amelia accept Harm and Jorge for who they are.'

'Yes, we do.'

'And that is what I want.'

Heather frowned again, this time in confusion. 'Surely if a female, any female, loves you, she will accept who you are.'

Matt was shaking his head before she'd finished talking. 'Not from what I have witnessed. Not all females cherish what makes their mates different.'

'You mean the fact you can fade? You think a female will find that abnormal?' Heather gently laughed. 'Matt, my friend, what you can do is abnormal.' At his hurt expression, she hurriedly continued. 'So what? All people, no matter what species they are, have differences, even abnormal ones.' She smiled and told him softly. 'They make us unique and are what attracts us to our mates.'

Matt nodded, then said. 'I am not like most other males.'

'No, you are not, but that only adds to what makes you, Matt, a kind, loveable, and exceedingly handsome male. And we cannot forget the Star Child gives us a mate to love and who will love us whatever our differences.'

Matt sighed with relief at the reminder of the Star Child. Then he grinned as he asked, 'May I tell Harm you called me exceedingly handsome?'

Heather stood and once more began scanning him. 'You can if you want to.' With a twinkle in her eyes, she told him. 'I have no problems with the way he assures me he is the only handsome male I should look at.'

Matt laughed, 'I am sure you do not. Thank you, Heather.'

She shrugged. 'It's what I do for friends. Now, how are you going to find out who your mate is?'

'As to that, I know of only one ship that left orbit this morn and my friend Mayton was on board. So I will speak to him.'

Heather grinned. 'And ask him to do some snooping. I see.'

Matt rocked his hand from side to side as he teasingly replied, 'You say snooping. I say scouting.'

'Ha-ha.' As she closed down the scanner, she said. 'You are good to go and it appears as though your mating has not affected you yet, but if you feel any symptoms, notify me at once.'

'Yes, Heather.'

'Good,' she shooed him to the door, 'now go and do whatever it is you do and I will comm you to arrange dinner.'

'Okay.' He stepped down from the table and smiled as he made for the door, only stopping long enough to say, 'Thanks, Heather. See you soon.'

'You too.' Smiling to herself, Heather sat behind her desk to fill in his after-training report. As she did, she couldn't help but think about what kind of female had snapped up one of the most eligible bachelors on Prime. Then she laughed, thinking of Peyton when she found out. The falears were one of her favorite people, especially Matt. Heather felt sorry for the poor, unsuspecting female. Just as well she was off world.

FIVE:

Shade moved along the shadowed hallways, staying out of sight of anyone who could exit the offices. He stopped for a moment outside the room that housed the Tivna, sister to their Beloved, but after one long look, he moved on.

If he could not talk to the Beloved, how was he to talk to the Tivna? No, he shook his head. He would push on. There was only one way to find out if his bondmate would reject him, as his Pride had done, as his mother had done. He sucked in a harsh breath and let the words fill his mind, as his promised mate had done.

A shaft of pain cut through him as sadness filled his heart. Would the pain never go away? It had been yentas since she had joined with his mother and their Pride to drive him from his home and yet the betrayal still hurt.

Now though, his heart and needar felt lighter. He had a bondmate, something he believed would never happen to him. Shade grinned. Life was definitely going to be different from now on. He would no longer be alone, searching for a reason to wake up each morning. Nor would he spend endless hours trying to find the reason why he had been born with the afflictions that made him different. Unfortunately, none of that could happen unless he could find the room that housed his bondmate.

Shade stopped moving when a small female with long silver hair walked from an office. He faded into the shadows, becoming undetectable. But as she neared his position, she stopped and whispered, 'Shade, he is not here. You will find him at the fourth Hex on the right. Good luck dearle.' She started to walk on then stopped and whispered a little louder, 'Oh, and you are expected at the Artar's for a check-up.' She turned her head and stared directly at him. 'And Shade, I will know if you do not go.' With a smile, she continued walking as if she had never spoken to him.

Shade did not acknowledge her or move. He was not even sure his heart was beating. Their Beloved had spoken to him, and not only spoken, she had known he was there and why. Joy infused him, making all the dim places in his needar fill with light. With a proud tilt to his head, he emerged from the shadows and raced for the Hex his Beloved had directed him to.

Once there, Shade studied the building. This one was not as open as the Beloved's residence. It seemed the males living here had secured the premises with electronic surveillance. The building was not impossible to breach; it was only a matter of deciding how he was to go about entering with least resistance.

Ahh! There it was, an opening. Granted, it was small, but with his unique abilities, the size was no obstacle. He sniffed at the small hole, tested it with a paw. There did not seem to be any security in this entryway, something he would have his bondmate examine and fix.

Using everything he had learned about his affliction, he morphed into a shaft of black light and slipped through the hole to materialize in a small room filled with shelves and floor-to ceiling cupboards. Large containers were stacked against the walls. He wondered if this was what the terrans called a storage room. He sniffed several times, then sneezed heavily. Someone needed to do some dusting. He softly sniffed the floor, worrying he was standing in something disgusting and sighed in relief when he saw his paws were clean.

Most doors on Maikonia were equipped with wall touchpads for the bipeds, or floorpads for adult Prowlers and kits to use. He was pleased to see this room had one, although it looked unused. With a flick of his paw, he swiped the pad and when the door swished open, he swiftly moved into the shadows and silently padded along the corridor.

Several minutes later, he found the door to his bondmate's apartment. Shade sat in the hallway and stared at the door, thinking about what was going to happen. His heart was still filled with hope and his needar was still light. For the first time since he had been chased from his Pride, he knew what he was about to do was right. Releasing the breath, he had inadvertently been holding, he stood to announce himself when he felt someone behind him and if he was not mistaken, the fur on his neck was now standing upright. With blinding speed, he whipped around to confront the danger at his back, a growl erupting as he did.

Gently, Matt purred, 'Calm now, calm. I am no threat. I am sorry if I startled you.'

Who are you? How did you appear without me knowing?

Matt crouched down, so he was level with the suspicious Prowler, who he thought was more surprised than scared. 'I am Matt Karto. I live here.'

The fur on Shade's neck settled, but his heart was still hammering in his chest. *That does not explain your sudden appearance, Matt Kato.*

Matt grinned at the acerbic Prowler. 'No, I can see that. This is how it was done.' With that, Matt faded and then reappeared. He was pleased to see the Prowler stood his ground and had not backed up or started growling as some had done in the past.

Shade was amazed. His bondmate could fade just as he could. Was it possible he would not view his afflictions as wrong? Before he thought too long about it, he said. *I am Shade; I am for you.*

Matt stood in surprise. He had only wanted to comfort the Prowler and now here he was reciting the binding that would unite them together forever. 'I am Matt Karto; I am for you.'

Shade blurted out before he thought overly long about what he wanted to say. *I have issues.*

Matt raised an eyebrow as he stared down at his bondmate. 'Issues? What would they be?'

Shade sighed and looked away from Matt. He did not want to burden his bondmate with his troubles. But that spark of hope flaming in his heart said he should tell him. Before he could form the words, Matt ran his hand down Shade's back in his first ever caress. *I… I…*

'It is alright Shade, I also have issues.' Taking a gamble that he was right, he stated. 'Once, I thought my abilities were afflictions given to me by an uncaring Star Child.'

But you do not think that now.

'No, I am grateful for what I can do. I have the abilities to safeguard our home and our people.'

Shade hesitantly stated. *And the Beloved.*

'Yes. She keeps us all safe because I and others like me were created to do what we can to protect her.'

Startled, Shade tossed his head at the thought of others like Matt. *There are others like you?*

'Yes, I will introduce you to them later. But for now, I sense you are needed elsewhere.'

I am. Gratefully, Shade grabbed at the chance to regain some sense of normality. To discover that someone else had abilities, he tasted the word ability and realized it was a word he enjoyed saying. It implied he was special, not damaged. He looked up at Matt, who waited patiently for him to say something and thought his bondmate would wait an eternity for him to speak. *I have an appointment with the Artar.*

'Are you unwell?' Matt demanded as he ran his hands over Shade's body.

Shade once more stilled at the touch of Matt's hands. *Ahh, I do not think I am, but I know I must go to the Artar.*

Matt listened to the tone of his voice and smiled. 'Did you happen to meet Madam Peyton before coming here?'

I am not sure how she knew I was there, but yes, she advised me I needed to visit the Artar.

'I see.' Matt gave him one last caress then softly asked. 'Shade, my bondmate, do you have abilities like me?'

Shade went to hang his head as he did when asked directly about his afflictions, then remembered Matt had called them abilities. He lifted his head proudly and stared Matt in the eyes and replied. *Yes, bondmate, I have.*

Matt smiled. 'Okay, let's go to the Artar and on the way we can discuss what abilities you have and I will tell you what mine are. I will also explain what I do for our world and our Beloved.'

SIX:

Echo and Relic traveled on the Battlecruiser, named Intercessor. Echo was extremely proud of her ship's name even when Relic stated in no uncertain terms it was a ridiculous name to call a Battlecruiser. She preferred something along the lines of Destroyer or Death Bringer... names that were totally inappropriate for a Battlecruiser belonging to the Star Daughter's Negotiator. Which Echo told her when she reminded her it was her ship and she could call it whatever she liked. This response, as predicted, ended with them on the mat beating each other black and blue.

It took them two days to travel to the small planet called Otera Minor. And when they made orbit, the Commander of the Battlecruiser informed her the time was 01:00 hours. Echo decided to wait until later in the morning to announce their arrival. So, with a smile, she bid her people a good eve and went to bed to sleep until Relic woke her by pounding on her door.

'Wake up, lazybones, you slept in. We have people to terrorize.'

Relic smiled when she heard cursing and then Echo yell. She danced along the passageway and had almost made the corner when she heard Echo scream.

'What did you do?' asked Avery as she leaned against the wall. Relic laughed, then told her, 'I told her she slept in and may have implied we were late.'

'Stars, no wonder she sounds pissed. It's barely 06:00.'

Smirking, Relic agreed. 'I know, I do love listening to her cursing first thing in the morn.

Avery shook her head. 'You sisters have the same kind of relationship as Peyton and her sisters.'

'Bite your tongue, female. We are nowhere near as bad.'

Avery smirked this time as she said, 'Keep protesting all you want. You know it's true. Your poor mates, they have no idea what they are getting themselves into.'

'Well, as neither of us have mates yet, there is nothing for anyone to be worried about, now, is there?'

Avery pushed herself off the wall as she thoughtfully looked at Relic. 'Hey girl, have you met your mate?'

Relic sighed and started to run a hand through her hair, then remembered it was braided in a warrior's braid. Her hand dropped away as she shrugged. 'Maybe. I think I have, only—'

'Only what?'

'Only, I'm not sure he feels the same way.'

'Oh, I see,' Avery grimaced, 'yeah, I know that feeling.'

Relic shrugged, then slung an arm around her friend. 'Come on, let's eat.'

'Eating won't cure what ails us,' Avery admonished.

'And yet it will go a long way to making us feel better.'

'Especially if there are hotcakes.'

'Mmm, hotcakes.'

'Relic, are you drooling?'

'Shut up.'

SEVEN:

Two hours later, Relic was standing next to Echo as she ordered, 'Wake them up.'

'Yes, Negotiator.'

Echo made herself comfortable at the head of the dining room table and asked Relic, 'How goes the search?'

'They just started.'

'How long?'

'Commander Gibson estimates fifty-five mins.'

'Why fifty-five?'

'It was the number she gave me.' Relic said as they watched the Warriors and healers leave the dining area to begin their search of the mansion's lower levels.

Captain Glenn added, 'Having five hundred Warriors, a Mystic and Scouts searching the world will ensure a quick result.'

Relic grinned. 'What the bright boy says is true.'

Captain Glenn Haughter was hand-picked by Kardan to join Relic's guard unit. He had wavered at first, hoping to be chosen to join a Warship where he could experience adventure and use his skills. But the Amahka had promised there would be plenty of adventures, and Commander Relic would add to the skills he already had. So far, he had been right. He stated with a humorous twist of his lips, 'You know I have a name.'

Relic murmured, 'And yet, I like bright boy.'

Echo grinned as she looked up at the young Captain. 'You know she says it with love.'

Glenn harrumphed in disbelief as he replied, 'She is just annoyed I won the poker game last night.'

Relic's growl was low and deep before she said, 'Because you memorize cards.'

'I do not. I am just a better player than you.'

Echo agreed. 'You know that is true, Relic. You suck at poker.'

'Typical, take his side.'

Glenn grinned as his ear-link pinged, alerting him to an incoming comm. Echo watched the Captain frown as he listened. 'Truth is truth, Relic. You know you are rash when you bet.'

'I'm telling you, he reads the cards.'

'Of course he does. You have to learn to work around that.'

Glenn finished his comm, still frowning as he told Echo and Relic, 'They have found males in the cells on the lower level.'

Echo stood as she said, 'Let's go see these males.'

Relic reminded her with raised eyebrows, 'What do want our Warriors to do with the people they are securing for you?'

Echo shrugged. 'Have the prisoners brought here. They can wait for us to return.'

'Prisoners! Is that not a little presumptuous?'

Echo grimly replied, 'Males found under the mansion. I think not, but if I am wrong, you can apologize for me.'

'Apologizing is not in my job description.'

'So you say.'

'I do.' Relic smiled with the others as she signaled her guards to surround Echo when she followed Glenn from the dining room.

EIGHT:

Relic looked around the lift as they made their way to the lower level of the mansion. 'They really like the colors gold and red.'

Echo agreed. 'They really do. It's everywhere, even in here, and this is a lift.'

A Terran Warrior on her first assignment with Relic's unit named Charis Piers, a dark-eyed, dark-haired beauty who topped Relic by three inches, said, 'Perhaps they think red and gold are the colors that depict wealth.'

Echo stated, causing Charis and Relic to smile, 'They would not be the first to think so. It is so sad they are wrong.'

Relic murmured, 'Maybe they don't get out much.'

Echo grinned. 'I suppose that could explain it.'

After exiting the lift, they walked along a corridor and came to a door marked with two crossed fists. Echo asked, 'What's behind here?'

Glenn opened the door and stated blandly, 'Cells.'

As they passed the empty cells, it was easy to see the fighters had been held against their will. Most of the cells had chains fixed to the walls and floors, a few had cots and not much more. Echo swallowed her anger before saying, 'I guess this is where they were held captive.' No one answered her, probably, she thought, because it was an obvious observation.

Glenn opened a door at the end of the hall and they walked into a large auditorium. He softy told her. 'They staged the tornays here.'

'I don't have a translation for that word.'

Relic told her, 'It means organized fights.' She grinned and replied to the question she could see in Echo's eyes. 'Reeve gave a lesson on tornays and what they entailed.'

Echo nodded as she looked around at the large auditorium. The floors and walls were a kaleidoscope of blood stains from fighters who had been forced to take part in the tornays held here. Warriors were helping males on to floaters. Most of them were wounded or undernourished and all were bruised or bloody. Several had untreated wounds, some even had missing body parts. None looked like they had seen a healer recently, if ever.

Several healers were running scanners over males leaning against the walls, while other Warriors talked quietly to even more males sitting on the floor. There wasn't a fighter who looked as though he had escaped some form of punishment.

Relic's hands trembled with the need to reach for the blaster on her hip. She badly wanted to return upstairs and kill every person responsible for this abuse. She asked Glenn, 'Is this all of them?'

'Yes Commander. A male said they were about to start morn training.'

Relic looked around. 'Okay, that makes sense. Why else would you be in here if you didn't have to be?'

Echo silently agreed with her as she watched a Warrior being helped on to a floater. From the corner of her eye, she saw a male sitting by himself. It appeared everyone was giving him a wide berth. She bet from the looks they were sending him; they'd had words and the healers were leaving him to either Relic or herself to talk to. This was confirmed when Glenn looked to see who had captured her attention. 'The healers have spoken to everyone but the Warrior sitting by himself. He has no belief we are here to help.'

Echo grinned at his diplomatic way of saying the Warrior had been uncooperative and had probably scared the healers. 'It's okay Glenn, I will speak to him.'

He looked away, then back at her as he said, 'They hoped you would. They do not want to sedate him. He is well liked by the other males, and they worry forcing him to take the drugs to subdue him will upset them.'

'Okay, let me see what I can do to prevent that.' Echo could feel the Warrior's eyes on her, and instinctively she knew this was someone she needed to know. 'Relic, do you believe in the gifts we have been given?'

'Of course, how else could we be here doing what we do for the Star Daughter?'

'So, if I say someone is important, you would believe me.'

Relic inclined her head. 'Always, Echo. Just as you would believe me.'

'Okay. That's good.' With a sign to her guards to stay where they were. Echo strolled over to the male and crouched down in front of him. 'Did you frighten everyone away?' He just stared at her without replying. With a grin, she asked, 'So you can't talk or just don't want to.'

He gave a deep growl of annoyance, then asked, 'Female, what do you want?'

'To know why everyone is stepping around you.'

'Because they are intelligent, unlike some.'

Echo looked up at Relic, a smile on her lips and worry in her eyes. 'Was that directed at me?'

Relic, hiding her grin, nodded. 'I'd say so.'

Looking the male over, Echo asked, 'Really, I don't understand it. You seem sweet to me.'

He barked out a laugh that grated on her ears and seemed to surprise him. Huskily, he growled, 'Amusing. Now leave me alone.'

'I am Negotiator Echo Wallace. You can call me Echo.'

'Can I now?'

'Yep.'

'Why would I do that?'

'Because I am pretty and males always want to do things for pretty females.' She smiled winsomely at him.

He just stopped himself from snorting at her ridiculousness. 'I don't see any pretty.'

'Well, it is there.'

'If you say so.'

'I do. Of course, I am not as pretty as my sister, Relic.' She pointed to Relic standing to the side of them both.

He moved restlessly, indicating he was in pain or just uncomfortable. 'Can only see you, so cannot compare.'

'Blind, huh?'

As if the words were pulled from him against his will, he growled. 'Not so much blind as tunnel vision, or so the healer told me. Too many hits to my head.'

Echo nodded. 'Okay, so you had healers?'

He snorted. 'Not so much a healer as a person who could run a scanner.'

'So, before you frightened my healers away, did they tell you where we are from and who sent us?'

'No.'

'We will fix your arm and sight.'

Before he could stop himself, he snorted in disbelief.

Echo assured him, 'I vow we will. So what is your name?'

'Competitor 107.'

Echo drew in a breath as she fell onto her butt. 'No… furin hayda, no.' the male reached for her with his amputated hand, then stopped and grimaced instead. Echo's voice was harsh as she demanded, 'Never say that again. It is just wrong.'

Grimly, the male said. 'You sound offended.'

'I am. As you should be, how dare you allow them to reduce you to a number!'

'It's not like I had much choice, now did I?'

Echo opened her mouth to scold the Warrior then subsided as she gently said, 'I apologize. Of course not. What was your name?'

Relic said quietly. 'Echo, leave him alone. He might not have one or remember.'

Echo waved her hand as she told her, 'Bullshit. He remembers. He's just being contrary.' She focused on the male again. 'What is your name?'

With a small smile, he muttered. 'Your talk is strange. You use words I do not understand.'

'We use words from our native language.'

'Uh-huh.'

'So what is your name?'

The male sighed deeply, as though talking was an effort. 'That male is gone. He died when he lost his hand and his sight.'

'Oh, so you want to leave him behind? I understand that. But I have to call you something.'

'Why?'

'I like you.'

He barked out another laugh, which was not as harsh this time, then said. 'Is that so?'

'Why is that so hard to believe?'

'Just is. So, Negotiator, why don't you give me a name, seeing as it is so important to you?'

Relic groaned. 'You don't know what you are asking, Warrior.'

'Captain! That I remember. She doesn't like my number, so name me, female, then leave me alone.'

Relic shook her head as she mumbled just loud enough for the Captain to hear, 'That is never going to happen now.'

Echo smiled as she stared at the male. He was handsome in the same way Marlo and Larson were. Suddenly, a thought occurred to her. 'Do you know squad Daimond?'

'Why?'

'We know them.'

'Is that right?'

'Yeah.'

'Where?'

'On our home world. See that is another thing the healers would have told you. Now you will have to wait.'

'For what?'

'To learn everything that you did not learn from the healers. So, I am going to have you taken to the Battlecruiser.' She looked up at Relic and smirked as she told him, 'Which I named Intercessor.'

'There is a Battlecruiser?'

Echo blinked as she asked, 'How else did you think we got

here?'

'You are from Emperor Uthar?'

'Oh, no. He is gone. They are all gone.' She placed her hand on his good arm and ignored his flinch. 'There is a lot that has happened, which I gather you do not know about. So please go with the healers to Intercessor, where you will be treated and receive an explanation of what has occurred.'

'You are not from this Universe, are you?'

Echo smiled, 'No, and that will be explained as well.' Standing up, she dusted her pants off as Relic motioned two medics over.

The Warrior looked up at Echo and squinted as he asked, 'So, what is my name to be?'

Echo looked at Relic and asked, 'What do you think of Shaw Wallace?'

With a grin, she nodded. 'He suits it.'

Huskily, the Captain asked, 'Is Shaw Wallace a good name?'

Echo told him, 'It is the name of a courageous male from our world.'

Relic asked him. 'Captain Shaw, will you allow the healers to help you onto a floater?'

'Is that one of them beds?' he motioned to the floating beds with his good hand.

'Yes.'

He nodded, and Relic nodded for the two medics to come closer before he changed his mind. He gingerly stood as he asked Echo, 'Not that I care, but will I see you again?'

Echo grinned, not allowing him to see how pleased she was at his question. 'Yes, I will come to medical as soon as I am finished down here.'

He nodded again and allowed the medics to load him onto the floater. 'Echo.'

'Yes.'

'What you found here are only some held in captivity.'

Echo looked at Relic and Glenn, who had come to stand with them. 'What… where are the others held?'

'On their homeworld, Otera Major. The Emperor holds

tornays with the newer fighters. I heard whispers recently the Emperor traded several fighters for an Elite. The whispers also say he is no longer sane.'

Urgently, Echo asked him. 'When was he traded?'

'Several luneras ago.'

'Okay.' She placed her hand on his shoulder. 'I will make sure we find all the fighters and they are taken back to their home worlds or they can come home with us. The Elite, as well. And I promise I will make it so this never happens again.'

'They will kill you. The tornays create a lot of credits for the Emperor and his world. He has nothing to trade, just the tornays and his fighters. Too many credits for it to be allowed to stop.'

Echo moved nearer to the floater and just stopped herself from reacting to the smell from his untreated wounds. How she had missed the stench earlier, she did not know. Perhaps she had been downwind of the male. Fiercely, she promised him, 'It will be stopped because I and the Star Daughter say it will.'

'Star Daughter?'

'Yes, my new friend, Star Daughter, as well as the Amahka Elite.'

'Amahka Elite?'

'Yes, her mate. See, so many things for you to learn. But for now, know this, the Star Daughter and Amahka Elite demand this abhorrent treatment of people be stopped and I am here to ensure their will is done.'

Shaw looked at the feisty female and smiled, something he had not done for many yentas. 'You know, I think I will believe you.'

'Good, you do that. I will see you soon.' She nodded to the healers, and they moved Shaw from the room. 'Relic, tell Avery I will see her when I return to the Intercessor.'

'Of course.' Relic tapped her link and began speaking.

Echo looked around at the emptying room and told Glenn. 'Okay, let's go. There is nothing we can do here that is not being done.' With that, she led the others back the way they had come without stopping again.

Relic murmured as she strolled alongside her sister, 'You okay?'

'Not really, but I will be when I talk to the Emperor." She nodded to Glenn and said, "Glenn, please find out if this world is legitimate and is registered for tornays.'

'As you wish Negotiator.'

Relic arched her eyebrows as she asked Echo, 'I'm guessing it will not be a long chat with the Emperor.'

Echo walked into the lift; her voice flat as she said. 'You guessed right.'

When they exited the lift, Relic dropped back to walk beside Glenn. 'I think our Negotiator is unhappy.'

'I heard that.'

'Place the unit on standby.'

'Yes, Commander.'

NINE:

When they reached the dining room, seven people sat around the table. Most were dressed in daywear, a few in nightwear, and one female in nothing at all.

'Interesting,' Echo murmured to Relic, who smirked at the well-endowed female as she signaled her Warriors to disperse around the room. Like her, they knew the only important person in that room was Echo. She, Relic knew, would dispute that fact, but Reeve and Hawk had spent luneras drilling this knowledge into each of Echo's personal guards.

Relic grinned as she said, 'One could say that or they could just say entitled rich bitchre.'

'One could, I suppose.' Echo took her place again at the head of the table and spoke to the seven people, 'Explain to me why there were chained males in your cells?'

A female dressed in satin nightwear which barely covered her silver body looked at Echo, her eyes flashing with hatred as Echo asked, 'What is your name?'

The female sniffed loudly and turned away from her. Relic smirked as she read from her tablet in English, 'Lady Gittar, aunt to King Addan over there.' She pointed with her forefinger at a well-dressed male lounging in a chair halfway down the table.

Echo thought he looked pampered, but if you liked pretty males, he was definitely one. He had short black hair and a long face; his narrow oval eyes flashed the same amber color as his aunts although they did not hold the hatred hers did. His, if Echo was not mistaken, held humor. It appeared the King found their appearance in his home amusing. Relic stated, 'He is the Emperor's son.'

Echo asked, also in English. 'And the others?'

'The two males are his cousins, none with a title, and those two females next to them are their girlfriends.' She indicated the two young females who appeared to be in their mid-twenties sitting on either side of the young males.

'Really, girlfriends?' Echo asked with raised eyebrows.

Relic shrugged. 'No, they are whores, but you know—'

Echo nodded. 'And the naked one?'

'She is the King's only sister. Her name is Jillana. Kido believes she sees to the accounts for the Emperor. She is a screamer.'

'Why is she naked?'

'Refused to dress.'

Jillana's eyes also flashed amber hatred at Echo and Relic, who smirked again.

Lady Gittar finally asked in a voice that dripped disdain, 'What is the meaning of this intrusion into our home?'

Echo replied politely, 'I am Negotiator Wallace. I am here on behalf of the Star Daughter. You are in breach of her edicts, which were sent to every world after the grand meeting held at the Capital.'

One of the young, pretty males with pink hair and silver eyes scoffed. 'Impossible. There is no Star Daughter. There has not been a Star Daughter for millions of yentas.'

Relic switching back to Coalition General said to Echo, 'You know, that must be so annoying for her. I cannot imagine how many times she must have wanted to zap the nutoros for saying that.'

Echo drummed her fingers on the table. 'She has far more patience than I gave her credit for. I mean, he's only said it once and I want to kill him.'

'I know.'

'How dare you?' snarled the young male.

Echo growled, 'One more word and I will make good on my threat. Now shut up, sit there and look pretty.'

He snapped his mouth closed at the implied threat. The naked female went to speak but at a sign from the King also snapped her lips closed. Seeing the interaction between siblings, Echo told the Kling, 'I will only ask my questions once. Refusal to answer will result in your deaths.'

The smirk on the handsome King's face became more pronounced as he asked in a lazy drawl, which Relic thought would have made Marlo envious, 'Do you have any idea who we are?'

'Yes, and still you will die. I am here because the Star Daughter heard rumors there were Warriors here, and she was right. So again I ask, why did you have beaten and chained males in your cells?'

The King waved an elegant hand as though he was batting away a fly or an annoying question. Either way, the action set Relic's teeth on edge. 'Negotiator Wallace, we use them for staged tournats and tornays.'

Echo raised her eyebrows at the uncensored reply. 'By whose authority.'

He looked nonplussed for a moment, then smiled charmingly and said, 'Mine, of course. I hold the tornays.'

'Do you charge for these tornays?'

'I am not sure what you refer to?'

'What I am asking is, do you allow other fighters and spectators to come and participate in the tornays?'

'Yes I do. We hold regular tornays.'

'Do your clients pay for the privilege of attending or participating?'

He inclined his head, 'Yes.'

'And are the tornays sanctioned by the Star Daughter or registered with one of her representatives?'

He looked at his sister, who raised her delicate eyebrows and made a slight gesture which Echo thought meant no, or tread carefully. The King sighed loudly and asked with just a hint of disdain in his voice, 'I was under the impression the Star Child gave us autonomy to rule our worlds without their interference. Has this changed?'

Echo grinned. 'All worlds are autonomous within certain guidelines. Those guidelines were sent to the governing body of every world.' She held her hand up as he went to speak. 'Captain

Glenn, do you have an answer to my query?'

'Yes, Negotiator, the answer is no.'

'Thank you.' She smiled at the King and stated. 'I just received clarification from Maikonia if a request was made by you, King Addan, or your father to be a legal tournay world. None was received. So again, I ask, by whose authority do you hold tornays here?'

The King spread his hands, 'That question would be better asked of my father; he runs this world. My sister and I are only administrators for him.'

Relic smirked as she said in English. 'See how quick he was to throw daddy out the airlock?'

Echo grinned as she replied, 'I noticed that.'

Just then, the King's sister demanded in a hard shrill voice, 'I am cold.' She pointed at Glenn and demanded, 'You, Warrior, retrieve my clothes.' Glenn remained where he was and stared blandly back at her. The female rose and screamed, 'I said get my clothes now!'

Echo rubbed her ear and said to Relic, 'I see what you mean. Sit down, Lady Jillana, and shut up. You were given time to dress, you chose not to. So now you will wear what you have on.'

'I am cold.'

Echo shrugged, 'Don't care.'

'But—'

Echo ordered, 'Gag her.'

Charis and another Warrior grabbed the female, who screamed as they roughly took her to the floor. In seconds, she was cuffed and gagged. Echo leaned back in her chair as the Warriors non-too-gently placed the now bound and still naked Lady Jillana back in her chair.

'How dare you!' spluttered the older female as she pushed back her chair and stood. 'She is the daughter of Emperor Alinac Zesiro.'

Echo nodded, 'I know.'

The King also rose and demanded, 'Release her now. This is outrageous!'

Echo said as she stood bringing all her guards to attention, 'What I find outrageous is how you have ignored your Star Daughter's demands for the return of her Warriors.'

The King flung his hand out toward his sister, ignoring everything Echo had just said, 'She is my sister. You have no right to do this.'

'What point are you trying to make?'

'You cannot treat us like this, this is our world.'

'Did you miss the part where I told you I am the Negotiator for the Star Daughter?'

'That does not give you the right to treat us like common criminals,' complained the King.

'Ahh, yeah it does. Now sit down or end up like your sister.'

Slowly, he regained his seat as his aunt pulled her chair forward and also sat. The King cleared his throat then stated, 'I demand you tell me what you intend to do with us.'

'Shut up nutoro, I have no time for your demands. Commander, have them taken to the brigg. We leave when the searches are complete.'

Relic replied, 'Yes Negotiator.'

'Okay, I am leaving.' Echo walked from the dining room without another word to the prisoners. She made her way to the shuttle, aware Relic and her guards followed at a distance. She stopped when she came to the shuttle's ramp and sighed as Relic asked from behind her, 'You want me to allow her to dress?'

'Nope, she can stay like that.'

'Harsh and chilly.'

Echo sighed again. 'I see it as justice. She is a bitchre as you said. Also, she loves the idea of being naked. She hopes it will shock us. Sad for her, it does not, although you should have her gag and restraints removed.'

Relic waved her hand down her own body as she asked, 'You aren't concerned the males will, you know—'

Echo grimaced as she turned her head to look at her sister, 'Eww really, with that woue. Our males have better taste. But if you are worried, have Charis and the other female Warriors escort her to the brigg and make sure there are one or two blankets there.'

'So benevolent.'

'I know, that's me. I am all heart.'

Laughing, Relic asked, 'I will make sure it is done. Where are we going now?'

'It is time to visit the Emperor and return his family to him. And I have to make my report.'

'Oh, fun for you.'

Echo snorted as she entered the shuttle. 'At least it's only to Bendrix.'

Relic grinned as she ordered the guards, 'Go help Captain Glenn, and then return to the Intercessor.'

'Yes, Commander.'

As she settled in her seat and strapped in, she told Echo, 'I have to report to Kardan.'

'Lucky you.'

Smiling, she murmured, 'Yep.'

TEN:

Once on board, Relic left Echo to make her report and see to her people. Echo wandered into medical delaying for a few minutes making her own report. 'Greetings, Avery, how is everything?'

Avery Finlay smiled, 'Greetings, Echo, nice to see you. We are good.'

Echo rubbed her face as she asked, 'So what are the numbers?'

'We have the fifteen Warriors from the mansion. Commander Gibson's Warriors found a further twenty in other parts of the city and there are seventy-nine non-warriors.'

'Are the searchers finished?'

Mayton Norr stated from behind them, 'They are doing a last sweep now, Negotiator Echo.'

Turning to confront him, she smiled as she gave him the once over. Harm had chosen Mayton to command the scouts but had made her promise to watch over him. 'Good, are you well?'

He nodded. 'I am. Do you need me for anything?'

'No, thank you.'

'Then I am away to write my report.'

Echo asked Avery as she watched the healer watch the Captain walk away, 'You should do something about that.'

'I want him to make the first move.'

'He won't. He is shy.'

'Oh, how do you know?'

'Kerol told me, and Avery, there is nothing written anywhere that says you cannot make the first move. It's not fair to leave it up to the Warriors all the time.'

She smiled. 'I guess that is true. I thought he may not be interested.'

'What... in you? Get over yourself female, you are beautiful.'

Echo was not lying. Avery was enchantingly beautiful with her pixie face surrounded by shoulder-length hair the color of bark, her hazel eyes sat behind thick black lashes and always held equal parts humor and intelligence. She was what Echo's mother would have called petite and Relic labeled dainty, even though she stood as tall as both Wallace sisters. Echo often saw females giving her envious looks when she wasn't watching.

Avery fluffed her hair and asked, 'So, you think I have a chance?'

Echo grinned as she placed an arm around the healer. 'More than a chance. I saw how he looked at you.'

With a million-watt smile gracing her face, Avery said, 'Alright then. Thanks, Echo.'

'My pleasure. Now, what can you tell me about Captain Shaw?'

'I can do better than tell you. I can show you.' Avery led her to a room that was occupied by ten regen units. Shaw was in the fifth one from the door.

Echo stood at the end of the tube and asked, 'How is he?'

Avery read the report on the regens comp. 'His eyesight has been restored and as you can see, his hand is almost completely regrown. Several of his organs were severely damaged and are being repaired now. All the infections have been isolated and the wounds treated. You have time to shower and make your report before he wakes. I gather you want to be here for that.'

'I do and thanks, he is important.'

Avery tried not to scrunch her nose up as she hesitantly asked, 'He's not your—' she shrugged uncomfortably, 'you know?'

Echo shook her head quickly and gasped. 'Dearle stars, no, what made you think that?'

Defensively, Avery muttered, 'You seem very interested in him.'

'I am, but sheesh, not for that.'

'Well, don't get all huffy. It was just a question.'

Echo shook her head. 'And you a healer, it's just tragic how your mind works.'

Laughing, Avery flapped her hand dismissively at Echo, 'Oh, go away.'

'I will, see you for eve-meal.'

Avery smiled. "Yes, unless I get up the nerve to talk to Mayton.'

ELEVEN:

After her shower, Relic dressed in loose black pants and a burgundy shirt, the outfit made her appear around fifteen years old. She ran a brush through her hair as she sat at the desk and stared out the large window Lady Brenda had insisted be installed in all the cabins.

It had been three luneras since they'd returned from the Capital. Sometimes she thought her life since their escape from earth was a dream. Then she would look around and realize she and Echo were really in another Universe serving an Entity known as the Star Daughter, and she had never been happier. Chuckling to herself, she thought if their mother could see them now, using all the skills they had learned on earth and some they had not even known they knew. She would be overjoyed to know her girls were surviving out here with Peyton and the others.

Thinking of her mother brought the grief that was never far away to the forefront of her mind, but thanks to Jarrod, it no longer left her paralyzed with anger. Now she could look back on that time and see it for what it was, just a memory. Most times it seemed like it happened thousands of years ago, and sometimes like now, it was as though it was only yesterday.

Avalon Wallace was a true descendant of the famous Scottish Knight, William Wallace. This lineage, Relic believed, was why her mother had an unconventional way of looking at life. It was no surprise to either sister when they learned their father was a conglomerate of genes selected by Avalon to give her daughters the best possible future.

At times, Relic believed her mother knew of the virus long before the virus decimated the world. Perhaps it was her study of the past that made her so in touch with the present and why she had her daughters educated as she did. Regardless of what it was, she made sure, along with a normal education, her daughters were schooled in all forms of martial arts and weapons. Avalon was convinced, self-defense was as important as reading, writing, and arithmetic.

Echo and Relic were up for the challenge, eventually surpassing all their teachers. Combat training formed their view of the world and taught them to compartmentalize their emotions. To raise a weapon against a foe was a serious and deliberate act of violence. One, they knew, that had lifelong consequences. Their mother often told them taking a life would weigh heavily on their hearts and souls as they walked through life and they believed her. Although this did not stop them from exacting revenge when they discovered their mother's killers.

One of Darby's data collectors had contacted their mother when they had been reaching out to groups of women, telling them about Peyton's great exodus from earth. Avalon had placed their names on the list and promised they would get themselves to Runnerdale in plenty of time. Then she had reached out to her daughters, who were working for the Powers group in different parts of the world.

After their mother told Relic and Echo of Peyton's plans, they arrived within days of each other, to a town close to Runnerdale. When three days passed without a word from Avalon, they knew something had prevented her from meeting them. Both sisters reached out to people they knew, but when their contacts produced no word of Avalon's whereabouts. Relic contacted the Powers' group, who promised to either locate Avalon or discover who had seen her last. When two days passed and no word came from the group or their mother, they knew something terrible had befallen her.

Unfortunately, when the group finally got in touch with them, it was to confirm their suspicions. Avalon was dead. She had been killed two days after contacting her daughters. Needless to say, neither sister left when Peyton and the others did. Instead, they began the hunt for their mother's killers. It took them several months to piece together why she was murdered and who was responsible.

It seemed that after contacting her daughters, Avalon reached out to her lifelong friend but could not find her. This was worrying because her friend was a chemist. It was possible she'd been picked up by the government in one of their sweeps for scientists, which happened often in those days, especially since scientists were mysteriously going missing. The sisters were to learn later those scientists had been rescued by Melody and her Warriors.

Unfortunately, that would have been better than what actually happened to Avalon's friend. She had been kidnapped and taken to a secret laboratory that was making a synthetic version of the drug Shosole. When she found this, she took matters into her own hands.

Relic thought, and not for the first time, if her mother had just talked to her or Echo, she would not have lost her life. The rescue attempt was poorly thought out. Probably, as Echo said more than once, because their mother's blood would have been hot and common sense would have taken a backseat to Avalon's anger. Regardless, the rescue attempt resulted in not only Avalon's death but her friend and four other women dying.

Within weeks of discovering what happened to their mother, Echo and Relic raided and destroyed five laboratories which were producing the drug and exposing several corporations and government ministers who were funding the laboratories. Needless to say, the sisters permanently retired the government ministers and anyone else associated with the corporations, be they executives, shareholders, alien or human.

While the world tried to recover from learning of the government's involvement with corporations manufacturing Shosole, Echo and Relic felt they had done all they could to keep people safe and avenge their mother. With the assurance from the Powers' organization that they would monitor any rumors of new laboratories being established and then remove them if found to be true, the sisters jumped on the first ship leaving earth, which unfortunately was a slave freighter. It had not taken them long to organize a rebellion and take over the ship. Eventually, they had met up with Charlotte, and the rest, as they say, was history.

Sighing, Relic closed the book on those thoughts and sent a kiss to the brightest star she could see. 'Miss you Mama, love you always.' She made herself coffee and asked Jax, 'Can you comm Kardan for me?'

'Of course. How was the meeting with the King?'

'Echo placed him and his family in the brigg.'

'Ahh, I see… Why is there a naked female in a cell?'

After taking a sip of coffee, she replied, 'She didn't feel the need to dress and Echo didn't feel the need to allow her to dress when she sent her to the brigg.'

'Amusing. Amahka Elite is ready.'

'Thank you, Jax. Greetings, Kardan, how are you this eve?'

'Greetings, Relic, I am well and you?'

Relic smiled, 'I am well so far. The mission was as we thought. Echo has detained the family and we are on our way to visit with the Emperor.'

As he studied Relic, Kardan couldn't help but think she and her sister Echo were more than just beautiful. It was as though their ancestry had added grace and intelligence to them both. If he was honest, he would admit their lineage fascinated him more than the actual females themselves. Since discovering they came from Warriors known as Knights, he had been studying who those Knights were, and what they were used for on earth. Much to Kardan's pleasure, Jax had discovered the Wallace legacy during his research. He wondered now if Matt knew of Relic's ancestry and what he thought of the Warrior blood she came from. Their mating was a development he was interested in seeing unfold.

Relic added, 'I will send you my report when I have written it.'

'Thank you. Is there anything urgent I need to know about?'

Relic grimace before admitting, 'One thing. It is possible there is an Elite, name unknown on Otera Major.'

Kardan's eyes sharpened at her words. 'Who told you this?'

'A Captain. He was a combatant here. He is in the regen now. I do not know his name and he cannot remember it or does not want to.'

'How does he know the Elite?'

'I cannot say, Amahka. I just know he has heard whispers that the male is on the Emperor's world and is insane or possibly insane.'

Kardan stared at her for a few minutes without speaking, then he asked, 'When do you arrive at Otera Major?'

'Two days.'

'I will meet you there.'

Startled, Relic squinted at Kardan and asked, 'Oh, okay... umm, why?'

'He is an Elite. He is by nature dangerous.'

'Oh, good point.'

Kardan restated. 'In two days, Commander.'

'Yes, Amahka.'

After Kardan's image faded, Relic sat sipping her coffee and stared out the window.

Finally, she muttered, 'Now, how the hayda am I going to tell Echo, Kardan is on his way. Dayam it!'

TWELVE:

Around the time Relic was reporting to Kardan, Mayton's was also making his report.

'Jax, comm Harm or Sedeen, please.'

'Certainly, Captain.'

Mayton was surprised when Jax told him neither Harm nor Sedeen was available for him to speak with, but suggested he talk to Matt.

Amused, Mayton agreed, 'That sounds okay, if Matt is available?'

'He is. I will connect you now.'

'Thank you, Jax.'

Matt grinned when he saw his friend. 'Mayton, how goes the mission?'

'Well, we have secured Otera Minor and are on our way to Otera Major.'

'How did your unit perform?'

'As expected, we had no casualties and no deaths.'

Matt pulled on his bottom lip. Mayton watched him and grinned. If he didn't know his friend better, he would say he had something other than the mission on his mind, which proved true when he asked, 'Good, good. So, I was hoping you could help me with something.'

'What can I do for you?'

Matt rubbed the back of his neck. Now he was going to ask Mayton, he felt nervous. Mayton almost spat his tea out when Matt said, 'I think my mate is on board your ship.'

Lowering his cup, he asked, 'What do you mean, you think?'

Matt grinned. 'That's just the thing. I sensed her here, then she was gone and your ship was the only one to leave Prime.'

'I see.' Mayton drummed his fingers on the desk. 'So by a

process of elimination you worked out she was terran and on board my ship?'

'Yep, that about says it all.'

'And you have no idea who she is?'

'None, not a clue.'

Mayton grinned slowly as he teased Matt. 'You falears always making things difficult, even with courting.'

Ignoring the lighthearted teasing, Matt asked, 'Courting? What is that?'

Heartlessly, Mayton said. 'Look it up. So a female on board my ship. Let's see… mmm, well, there are Charis and Cleo. That would be Cleo Gibson.'

'I know who she is, and no, it's not her or Charis. Wasn't there a healer as well?'

'Yes, and no, it is not her.'

Matt could see Mayton was serious. 'Why not?'

'She is taken already.'

'I see.' Matt grinned as he asked, 'Would that be by you, my friend?'

Mayton sighed. 'It would be if I could bring myself to speak with her.'

Concerned for his friend, Matt asked. 'Mayton, you are not denying her, are you?'

'No!' Mayton emphatically responded. 'I just… hayda Matt, I just don't know what to do.'

Understanding lit Matt's eyes. 'I know. I, too, feel that way, but as we have seen, if we do nothing, we will go insane and I fear that is not an option. As much as we would like to hide there for a while.'

Mayton laughed. 'You are right, I will speak with her.'

'Excellent. Now for my problem. If it is not your mate nor the Warriors, that leaves—'

Mayton's eyes sparkled with mirth as he interrupted him, 'The Wallace sisters.'

Matt hung his head and mumbled just loud enough for Mayton to hear, 'That way is fraught with danger.'

Laughing, Mayton shook his head. 'They are not desouls, Matt, you can do this.'

'No, they are not, but they are well liked by Peyton and her sisters.' He sighed heavily. 'I am doomed.'

'I feel for you, but there are other possibilities. I will send you the personnel list.'

Matt grimace. 'Do so, but you know as well as I do, it will not be anyone else but one of the sisters.'

As Mayton disconnected, he thought maybe Matt was right.

THIRTEEN:

Once she was finished with her shower, Echo sat at her desk to make her own report to Bendrix. 'Jax, comm Bendrix please.'

'Certainty, Negotiator.'

'Please call me Echo. I know you call my sister by her first name.'

'I do, and thank you for inviting me to do so.'

Echo grimaced, 'I should have done so before now.'

'It is of no concern Echo. We all forget social niceties on occasion.'

'Are you taking classes in manners from Relic? Because, regardless of what she tells you, not everything is about politeness. Sometimes bluntness is the way to go.'

She could hear the amusement in his voice when he replied, 'Not just your sister. Madam Peyton, often instructs others in social behavior.'

'Since when?'

'All the time.'

Echo snickered at his dry tone as she mocked, 'I feel so sorry for her students. Relic is bad enough.'

Echo was sure she heard a smile in his voice when he told her, 'Ambassador Bendrix is ready for you.'

'Thanks, Jax.'

'You are welcome.'

'Greetings, Echo. How is everything?'

'Greetings, Bendrix. Things went as predicted, except for the fighters we found.'

While Echo continued with her report, Bendrix studied her. As always, when confronted with Echo, he thought for a terran she was a beautiful female. Not as beautiful as his Netta, obviously, but still attractive enough to make a male give her a second glance. Which was an expression he'd overheard Gunner say to Mark about the Wallace sisters. Mark had replied that it was like looking at exotic flowers that finally bloomed. Bendrix agreed with that description as well.

Over the last three luneras, he had seen glimpses of this female who spoke so eloquently about what she had seen, felt and hoped to accomplish when she arrived at Otera Major. He smiled to himself as he realized Peyton had once again won the bet. Echo Wallace was born to be a Negotiator. When she finished speaking, Bendrix remarked, 'It appears you used your discretion well. Although the naked female may be stretching that a little.'

Echo grinned. 'Possibly, we will see.'

On a serious note, he asked, 'It may be necessary to remove the Emperor and his family from Otera Nobel. Are you prepared for this?'

Echo was unconcerned by his warning. 'Bendrix, you should know by now I am prepared to go the distance. And after what I have seen today, they should hope they are only removed.'

Bendrix shrugged, a mannerism he had picked up from Netta. 'As always, the decisions are yours. Just remember, every decision you make has consequences. Not only for the world and its people, but for you and your needar.'

'In other words, remember I have to live with myself afterwards.'

Bendrix agreed, 'Yes, something I feel this Emperor needs to be reminded of.'

Echo nodded grimly, thinking of Shaw and the Elite held in captivity. 'Yes, he does.'

Bendrix asked for formality's sake, rather than he thought she had forgotten to tell him. 'Anything else to report?'

'No, that's it.'

'Then I wish you good hunting and look forward to your report after your visit to Otera Major.'

'Thank you.' As the holo-screen shut down, Echo looked out the window and ran through all the potential scenarios of what waited for her on Otera Major.

FOURTEEN:

The newly named Shaw Wallace looked around at the blue sky with one yellow star and asked, 'Where the hayda am I now?'

'Welcome to my world or what passes for it.'

Shaw looked over at the small female with long silver hair and startling blue eyes. She looked like his Echo. 'Do I know you?'

'I suppose you do, in a way.'

'So, this is where?'

'The Kail would say we are in my mind, but truthfully, we are on another plane of existence where I can construct,' she spread her hands 'this world.'

Shaw let the reference to another male go and asked instead, 'Why do you do so?'

Peyton shrugged as she walked to the rocking chair waiting for her on the front porch of her grandparents' home. Shaw watched her from narrowed eyes and saw the glow that surrounded her. His gift was to see the needar of any being, be it good or bad. Something inside of him wanted to jump for joy at finding the Star Daughter. The more cynical side of his nature asked why now? So he did what he always did and kept his feelings hidden.

He looked at the white picket fence running along the property line and then down at his feet. Curious, he crouched and ran his hands over the green spiked plant he was standing on.

Peyton reached the porch and turned to see why the male had not followed her, and smiled. 'On my world we call that grass. It is a plant that covers the ground. We think it looks pretty.'

Shaw nodded, then hurriedly stood as a low hum vibrated against the soles of his shoes and was followed by a low flat purple disk. 'What is that?'

Peyton laughed. 'Oh, I forgot about that. We call them lawn bots. It keeps the grass cut to the length I like.'

'But if this is a construct, why does it grow?' Huffily, Peyton asked, 'What is your point?'

'Just seems like an unnecessary vanity to me.'

Peyton's eyebrows rose as she took her seat and shoved the rocker a little harder than she intended. 'Is that so? And you know so much about vanity?'

'I have studied it up close and personal, so to speak.'

'Do you know who I am?'

Shaw saw the sparks in her needar and carefully replied, 'Am I supposed to?'

Peyton saw the lie, and the caution he used to answer her, and regretted her spurt of temper. This is what happened when Kardan told her he was leaving for a few days. She got all unbalanced. Perhaps she should take the trip to visit the Haffee family and talk to their planet Souviss. They had waited long enough. Satisfied with her plans, she gently said. 'No.'

She eased off on the rocking and motioned for him to join her on the porch. Shaw gingerly sat in the chair next to hers. The chair moved as Peyton told him, 'I am not liking the name Shaw. It's not right for you.'

Shaw looked out past the gate and stated simply, 'She gave it to me.'

With a smile, Peyton told him. 'Echo, yes, I know.' She looked sideways at him and said. 'Echo is seldom wrong but in this she is incorrect.'

Shaw silently agreed with her. He had known the name was wrong the moment Echo had spoken it. 'I, too, think the name is not mine.'

Peyton hummed, then murmured, 'Wallace she should keep for her own young. Shaw you should keep, although it is not enough for who you are and for who you are to become.'

Confused and intrigued by what she said, Shaw looked at the small female and whispered. 'Is it not? So what name should I take?'

Peyton's eyes filled with the stars of the Universe as she took his hand and breathed a name. 'Judge.'

'What name is this?'

Releasing his hand, she explained. 'It is from my birth planet. It means one who sees the truth of a person. Someone who is worthy to make a judgement on others.'

A smile escaped as he asked, 'I see, and you think I am worthy of this name?'

'I know you are more than worthy and will prove so in the future.'

'So, you are a Sene now?'

Peyton smiled again. 'I am many things. Will you wear the name?'

'I will take the name as mine.'

Peyton relaxed back in her chair. For a minute she had thought he was going to refuse, which would have destroyed all her and Echo's plans. 'Shaw, will make a good family name and it will make the sisters happy.'

The cynical side of Judge raised its head as he demanded to know, 'And that is important to you?'

'Oh yes, most important. Just as you are.'

'Why? I am just a Warrior and not a good one at that.'

Peyton twisted her body, so she was looking directly into his eyes as she told him, 'That is a lie. You have protected your Elites. Even now you say nothing of where they are.'

Judge jerked at the mention of the Elites. 'I have not thought of them for many yentas.'

'Do not now. Someone will come soon, and you will remember where they are. There is time to save them all.'

'Is there? I fear too long has passed already.'

Peyton assured him, or maybe she was hoping to reassure herself, 'There is time.'

Judge nodded and asked, 'What am I to do now?'

'You will heal and then an entirely new future will open for you. One which I think will be unexpected but worthy of all your gifts and hard-won experience.'

'Do I still have a choice?'

'Always. There is always a choice. You just have to find what it is.'

'For me and those in my care.'

'As it has always been.'

'Perhaps—'

'Hush now, return to sleep. All will be revealed in time.'

'Should I—'

'Sleep my Warrior, sleep.'

FIFTEEN:

Judge Shaw came around slowly and sighed when his heart faltered, as it always did on waking. It was only as the silence and scent of cleanliness impinged on him; he realized something was different. He was not hearing the anguished cries of the hopeless or feeling the rage of his fellow Warriors. There were only the soft sounds of machines and even quieter footfalls.

Opening his eyes, he blinked furiously as light and shapes bombarded him. Instinctively he flung his arm over his eyes to protect them. Then it was as if everything stopped, even his heart slowed. The only thing he could feel was his hand touching his face. Slowly, as if the Universe wanted him to realize a miracle had occurred while he'd been asleep, he raised his arm and stared at his hand. Instinctively he counted five fingers. Unable to believe his eyes, he ran his other hand up and down his new arm and then touched each of his fingers.

'It is real,' said a voice he was positive he had only dreamed. He turned his head on the pillow and stared at the beautiful female sitting in an armchair by his bed. She passed him a tube of orange liquid and smiled. 'This is a protein drink. Healer Avery says you will need several of them over the next few days because of the regen.'

Sitting up, he took the tube and mumbled, 'I know you.'

'Yes, we met earlier.'

'I have been altered.'

'You received the download all our people who return home receive. It allows you to understand Terran and other languages. Also, it gives you information about our homeworlds, and the Star Daughter and Amahka Elite.'

He took the tube in his newly restored hand and said, 'Not only within my mind.'

'No, your mind was not the only thing altered. Your body is whole again, although undernourished, hence the drinks.'

Judge nodded, then blurted, 'I wish to thank you for the name you gave me, but I have decided I would like the name I have chosen.'

Confused, Echo asked, 'When did you choose a name?'

'While I slept. I dreamed of a beautiful female who gifted me with a name.'

'Oh okay. Did the female have a name?'

'She did, but I cannot recall it.'

Echo smiled. 'No matter. So, what name have you chosen?'

'I have offended you.'

'Nah, I am happy you want to pick your own name.'

'I will keep Shaw, that I feel suits me.'

'Okay. So what do I call you?'

'Judge.'

'Judge? What kind of name is Judge?'

Judge grumpily stated, 'It is a good, strong name.'

Grudgingly, Echo agreed. 'Judge Shaw, yeah, it's okay. Not as good a Shaw Wallace, but okay.'

Judge told her, 'You will name your son Wallace. It is a good name.'

'Whatever, no pressure.'

'Not that you will be mating anytime soon.'

Huffily, Echo asked, 'Why the hayda not?'

Judge simply stated, 'No one will be worthy of you, that is why.'

Echo's mouth dropped open and then snapped shut. 'See, this is getting out of hand already.'

'Oh my stars, you are not fighting with the poor male, are you? He has just been healed.'

Echo and Judge looked over to see Relic standing with her arms crossed, glaring at Echo.

'He changed his name.'

Relic opened her eyes wide. 'Why... what was wrong with Shaw Wallace?'

'He says he's more a Judge.'

'Who?'

Judge stated defensively, 'Judge. I like it.'

'What kind of name is that?'

Echo nodded, 'I said the same, but he said he dreamed of a female who gifted him the name. Although, he is keeping Shaw.'

Relic hummed, then relented, 'You cannot argue with that, and it is his name.'

Judge nodded as he told Echo, 'You were right when you said your sister is prettier than you.'

Echo muttered, 'No need to be nasty.'

Relic fluffed her hair. 'Get over it, you know I am.' She told Judge, 'It is my curse to bear.'

Judge's eyebrows rose in reply, causing her to grin and Echo to snort in disbelief at her sister's audacity.

When she had come looking for Echo, Relic had been unsurprised to see her sitting by Judge's bed. She wondered about the female in his dream, because Judge was very much a terran name. But as she looked at the healthy, although underweight, male, she decided he looked more like a Judge than he had a Shaw. She frowned as she looked closer. He looked a lot like Larson, and she wondered if he was related to him.

Unlike most Warriors, Judge had short, blond hair and a square-cut face with piercing black eyes and a brown ring. He was large or would be when he regained his weight, but even without it; he looked well-muscled. She tipped her head to the side as she stared hard at him.

Noticing, Judge asked, 'Why do you look so?'

'It's just that you look a lot like our friend's mate.'

'Who would that be?'

'Larson Sillva.'

He whispered the name several times before saying, 'I have not heard that name for many yentas.'

'So, you know him?'

'I do. We were clutched together, then I was placed with my squad and he was placed with his. I never saw him again.'

Echo asked softly, 'Would you like to speak to him?'

Judge nodded as he cleared his throat. 'I would like that immensely, but not now. I need some time.'

'You need to adjust to your life now,' stated Mystic Ziven.

Echo smiled. 'Greetings Ziv, how are you?'

'I am well, Lady Echo, and you?'

'Good.'

'Commander Relic, you are well?'

'I am Ziv, thank you.'

The Mystic looked at Judge and smiled. 'I am Mystic Ziven Batara and I have come to discuss your new life with you.'

'Do I need to do this?'

'Yes, it is what all newly recovered Warriors do. It is a requirement of Kail Jarrod's.'

'So, we have no choice?'

'Usually there is always choice, but in this there is none given. I vow it will be beneficial and, in the end, you will be more |Judge Shaw than you were anyone else.'

Echo stood and grinned at the grumpy male. 'Cheer up, Judge. Ziv is one of the nicest males I have ever met.'

Relic told him, 'And the quicker you talk to him, the quicker you get to leave here and rejoin life.'

'They are both correct,' Ziven said as he sat in the now vacant chair. 'Ladies, we will see you for eve-meal.'

'Okay, see you both later.' Relic said as she took her sister's arm in hers.

Hesitating, Echo stated, 'Maybe I should stay, just in case.'

Relic told her, 'No… no, it doesn't work like that and you know it.'

They heard Echo say, 'so bossy' as they left the room. Ziven told Judge, 'They are delightful.'

Judge nodded, 'I find them so.'

Ziven smiled as he tried to gage the male's reaction to what he was going to tell him. 'Echo has a plan in mind for you.'

Judge smiled as he replied, 'I may not be fully functioning yet, but even I guessed that.'

'And you do not mind?'

'I assume I was not rescued to become someone's toy. I have choices now, as decreed by the Star Daughter.'

Ziven smiled as he agreed. 'Yes, you do, as we all do. Freedom is yours for the taking.'

'It is an intoxicating sensation,' Judge murmured as he held his arm up for Ziven to see. 'Just as this is.'

From there, Ziven led the talk to Judge's past and his hopes for the future.

SIXTEEN:

Two nights later, the Battlecruiser named Intercessor arrived at Otera Major. Echo called a meeting of her Commanders for a briefing with her tech people.

Her techies were mates, Kido and Haruto Nomura. They had been data collectors for Darby. But when this mission was posted in the Oracle, the couple couldn't volunteer fast enough. Kido told Echo she and Haruto preferred to travel than stay at home. When Relic told her the missions could be dangerous, she had smiled and said danger was her middle name. She then had to explain to her mate what that expression actually meant.

Haruto was a Graynite Warrior discovered with his squad brothers and other Warriors just before Peyton and her people left the Capital. Haruto had taken Kido's surname rather than combine their names. Kido was thrilled, as it meant her family name would survive into the future. For her, there was no better way to honor her ancestors.

Echo and Relic were not the only ones amused at the pairing of the diminutive Kido and her gigantic mate although no one was stupid enough to say anything to Kido. She was one of five instructors in the art of Iaido, a style of sword work that was not only deadly, but an art form.

Echo was pleased the couple were with her. Their ability to gather information and condense it into relevant points was invaluable. She hoped they would become permanent team members on the Intercessor.

Now, as everyone took their seats, Kido stood at the head of the table in the Battlecruiser's conference room. 'Greetings. This report will be short.'

Charis asked, 'Which we appreciate.'

Kido grinned as she stated, 'Thank you. Emperor Alinac

Zesiro rules Otera Major. He has remained unmated since the Empress passed away in childbirth over fifty yentas ago. He has two children, King Addan and Lady Jillana, who we have met. He has a sister, Lady Gittar, who we have also met, and a brother, King Baen, who we are led to believe organizes all the tornays, even the ones on Otera Minor, and acquires fighters for the Emperor. At the moment he and the Emperor are on world.'

Echo asked, 'Are they not always at home?'

'No, they are usually visiting other worlds or at the Capital.'

Relic asked, 'So why are they here now?'

'Because there is to be a major tornay in two wekens. Fighters from around the galaxy are coming to participate.'

Glenn asked, 'What is the prize?'

Kido looked at her mate who stood and bowed. 'From what I could ascertain, the prize is a planet and one hundred fighters of their choosing.'

'Excuse me!' Echo exclaimed. 'Are you saying if a fighter wins, he or she gets an entire planet and a stable of fighters?'

Haruto shook his head, 'Firstly, there are no female fighters and no, Negotiator, not the fighter. The fighter's owner receives the prize.'

Relic asked, 'What do you mean, there are no female fighters?'

Glenn stated solemnly, 'It is not done.'

'The hayda you say?'

Glenn smiled as he told her, 'I do say, Commander, this is not earth. Females are too delicate to take part in this male dominated contest.'

Echo snarled, 'The hayda you say.'

She stared at her sister, who burst out laughing, then stated, 'This is going to be fun.'

Echo sighed. 'Your sense of humor is faulty.'

Relic narrowed her eyes at her sister. 'You are not going to sit there and disagree with me, are you?'

'Well no. What would be the point?'

'Exactly.'

Charis asked quickly, 'What does the fighter get?'

Relic muttered, 'To live.'

Echo drew in a heavy breath and asked, 'Is that so?'

Kido nodded, 'It seems so.'

Echo shook her head and bit back on what she was going to say, instead asking, 'Anything else?'

'No, that is all.'

Relic said, 'One more question.' When she received a nod from Kido, she asked, 'Have they always held tornays here?'

Kido frowned as she scrolled her tablet, when she found what she wanted, she stated, 'No, only since Emperor Zesiro began ruling the world. That would be sixty yentas ago. It appears the world was in trouble when he took over. They had suffered a drought for near on a hundred yentas. The population had fallen as people died or left for other worlds. Eventually the government disappeared. Nothing says whether they died or were killed or just left. Eventually, the world became a haven for Raiders which reduced the population even more as people hurried to get away from them. The ones unable to leave became the unwilling victims of the Raider's games.'

Haruto said, 'This is where the Emperor stepped in. He arrived and chased the Raiders from the planet and has stopped them from returning. Coincidently, within six luneras after his arrival, the rains began.'

Echo laughed. 'I see where this is going. They considered him their savior. He arrives and the Raiders leave and the rains return.'

Haruto agreed with her summation. 'Yes exactly, and then the rains stopped again, and the people became distraught. They were concerned the drought had returned. So the Emperor suggested the tornays as a way of preventing starvation and the Raiders returning. The people agreed and here we are today.'

'Are the people still in agreement?' asked Echo.

'We are not sure,' Kido replied. 'A message was sent to the Capital asking for help which was then given to the Star Daughter. We are unsure how long ago the message was sent.'

Relic asked, 'Can we make an assumption as to why?'

'It seems the Emperor and his family have decided they no longer want the people of Otera Major to remain on world. They have been given two luneras to leave or they will be forced to fight.'

Relic asked before Echo could, 'What does he want to do with the planet?'

'Turn it into a world that promotes tornays.'

Confusion was the predominate expression on most of the faces of the people in the room, as Relic said, 'I don't understand.'

Kido flicked her tablet, and the wall became a screen. 'This diagram was smuggled out along with the message.' On the screen was a badly drawn map showing several arenas of varying sizes and what looked like high-rises similar to the ones at the Capital.

'As you can see, there are no homes or markets anymore. The high-rises are to house the dignitaries and spectators as well as the fighters and their owners or managers. The arenas are to be built so there can be different tornays, depending on the ability of the fighter. The tornays are open to amateur's right through to the experienced. Obviously, as they improve, if they improve, they will advance into a larger arena.'

Glenn asked, 'So as a fighter wins more fights, he or she gets better tornays and the owner receives more credits?'

Haruto was the one to reply, 'Yes, Captain, that is correct.'

Echo stated, 'Of course, the fighter has to survive or not get too injured so they can fight again.'

Haruto agreed. 'Otherwise, the fighter will end up here,' he showed them a picture of a large underground crematorium.

Echo tapped her fingers on the table as she said, 'Wonderful. Well, I don't know about all of you, but I think this needs investigating. At the very least, we will stop the removal of the people from their world. Kido, what is the population now of Otera Major?'

'At the last count, the population tallied just over one million.'

Relic mused out loud, 'The world hasn't grown in the last

sixty yentas, has it?'

Glenn asked, 'I wonder what stopped it.'

Charis was quick to say. 'Or who.'

'My credits are on the Emperor,' stated Kido.

They all laughed as Echo said. 'Ours, too.' Standing, she said, 'Alright, we will shuttle down just after dawn.' She looked at Kido. 'You and Haruto will remain on board until I require you both on world.'

'Yes, Echo.'

She looked at the silent Mayton Norr. 'Scout Commander, what are you and your unit doing?'

'We will go down tonight and meet you when you arrive.'

'Have you contacted the person Kardan gave you?'

'Yes, we are to meet her as soon as we land.'

Echo didn't bother asking Relic if she and her guards were ready. It would only annoy her, and she wasn't up to a fight. Instead, she asked the so far silent Commander who was to secure the planet, if she was ready. 'Commander Gibson, are you and your Warriors ready?'

Cleo Gibson was of average height and weight for a terran, which were the only average things about her. In everything else, she was exceptional. Her language skills were equal to Trina's, just as her shooting skills were equal to Melody's. She was as beautiful as Netta, with flashing green eyes and golden tipped shoulder length blue hair. It was hard to say what part of earth she came from, but if one was to guess, they would say Eastern Europe.

Cleo had joined the Armee as soon as she left earth and had risen within the ranks to make Commander two luneras ago. Hawk had recommended her for this mission. It was her first command and so far, Relic was impressed with her. Echo was reserving judgment until the end of the mission, but she hoped she did well and, as with Kido and Haruto, would remain with her. Cleo replied in her quiet way, 'I and my Warriors are ready.'

'Good, although there is a slight change in plans.'

Echo grinned as Cleo raised an eyebrow as she dryly asked,

'Really, Echo, what change have you made to the plans you and I took hours to formulate before we left Otera Minor?'

Echo just stopped herself from wincing. 'When you say it like that, it sounds bad.'

'Because it is bad.'

'But I have received new information since then.'

'I see. So, what changes do you wish to make?'

'Just one.'

'Which is?'

Serious now, Echo stated, 'I want you and your Warrior's securing the city where the Emperor lives before you secure the planet. I do not want him or anyone affiliated with him leaving the city.'

Cleo tipped her head back and stared at the ceiling. Relic knew she was going over the map of the city Kido had obtained. It was what she would be doing. Cleo asked Mayton, 'Can you and your unit help?'

'We can identify break points and relay them to you.'

Cleo told Echo, 'Yes, we can do that.'

'Good, so if there is nothing else, let's adjourn and meet in the morn.' With a nod to everyone, Echo left and within minutes was in her cabin. As she changed into her sleepwear, she asked Jax, 'What time is dawn on Otera?'

'In seven hours.'

'Okay, let's have everyone up and ready by then.'

'I will wake everyone an hour before departure.'

'Thank you, Jax.' Yawning, she fell into bed and was asleep minutes later.

Relic returned to her cabin, 'Jax, what is wake-up call?'

'Six hours from now.'

'Thank you.'

Relic also changed for bed and within minutes of her head touching the pillow, was asleep only to jerk awake sometime later when she realized she had forgotten to tell Echo Kardan was on his way to Otera Major. She thumped her pillow and growled, 'Dayam it, she is gonna be so pissed.'

SEVENTEEN:

Echo sipped her first coffee of the day, cursing Relic. She had woken early, hoping to scuttle her sister's attempt to repeat her early morn call and dayam it, it seemed she had outsmarted herself, because Jax told her Relic was tucked up in bed fast asleep.

A grin some may call evil crossed Echo's face. 'Well, I may as well make use of the time before we leave for the planet, seeing as I am awake and all.' Sitting at her desk, she asked Jax, 'Can you comm Commander Matt for me, please?'

'Certainly, Echo.'

Shade nudged his bondmate once more. *Wake.*

'Wh… what?'

Wake up, you have an incoming comm.

Scrambling for his clothes, he asked, 'Why are you telling me this?'

Jax tried, but you would not wake, so he asked me to.

Matt stopped tugging on his pullover and looked at his bondmate. 'I am sorry. Were you concerned?'

Shade admitted to the fear he felt when Jax told him he could not rouse Matt. *I was worried.*

'I should have explained, I sleep deeply when I have used my gifts.'

As we did yesterday.

'Yes. Are you not tired?'

No, should I be?

Matt gave his ears a soft caress. 'No, I am happy you are not.'

Jax interrupted their conversation to tell him that Echo was waiting to talk to him.

Matt asked, 'Echo Wallace, are you sure?'

'I am positive. Shall I open the comm?'

'Yes, give me a min to get to my study, please.'

Echo sipped her coffee as she waited and watched a few stars race by her window. Finally, Jax came back to her. 'I am waiting for him to reach his comp.'

'Was there a problem?'

'No, Matt sleeps deeply after he uses his gifts.'

'Oh, okay, just connect when he is ready.'

'As you will, Echo.'

'While we wait, I do have a favor to ask of you.'

'What would that be, my new friend?'

Grinning, she said, 'I was wondering if you could find these vids for me.' She typed in several titles on her comp.

'Yes, I can find them.'

'Once you find them, can you study them, please?'

'May I ask why?'

'It is for Matt and Relic. When you have watched the vids, I am sure you will understand.'

'Is it necessary for me to do this to help Relic?'

'Inadvertently. It is more to help Matt.'

'I may have questions.'

'Which you will direct to me only.'

'Of course. Matt is ready.'

Matt dropped into his chair at his desk as his comm chirped and Echo's face appeared on the screen. 'Negotiator, has something happened to Mayton?'

Echo frowned, 'Why, when anyone sees me, do they automatically think of tragedy?'

Matt grinned. If she was being snarky, then this was not about his friend. 'Perhaps it is because you seldom talk to anyone, so—' he shrugged, leaving the sentence hanging.

Echo grinned, erasing her frown. 'There is that. The thing is, I don't talk a lot because I have to do it as the Negotiator. So, I sort of get a little irritated at idle chatter in my personal life.'

Matt nodded in understanding. 'It is the same with me. I fade when I am scouting. I do not when I am off duty.'

Echo smiled at his explanation. 'Yes, exactly, although fading for fun seems like, well, fun.'

Matt's eyebrows rose as he asked, 'How so?'

Impishly, she said. 'Imagine playing hide and seek with you.'

Matt laughed at her observation. 'I have never thought of that.'

'Well, if you ever decide to have a game, I want to be on your team.'

'I will remember that.'

Shade, hearing his bondmate laughing, strolled into the room Matt called a study. He circled the desk to stand next to his bondmate and stare at the beautiful female on the screen. Automatically, Matt ran his hand down his back.

'Negotiator—'

'Please.' Interrupted Echo. 'Call me Echo.'

Matt inclined his head. 'Echo, may I introduce my bondmate Shade?'

'Greetings, Shade.'

Greetings, Echo, it is nice to meet our Beloved's Negotiator.

'As it is to meet you.'

Matt finally asked, 'What can I do for you, Echo?'

'May I be blunt?'

'Please do, it is early morn here.'

Echo grinned at the answer. 'Are you my sister's mate?'

'I believe I am.'

'You do not sound positive.'

'I knew my mate was on board the Intercessor but until now I was unsure who it was.'

'Now you know it is Relic?'

'Yes.'

'And you are okay with that?'

Matt frowned as his hand stilled on Shade. 'Why should I not be?'

'Matt, this is my sister. She has known for luneras you are her mate, so you see where I am going here?'

'No, no, I do not. Please explain.'

Echo shrugged. 'She is Relic and when it comes to her

personal life, she is a jumble of anxieties and doubts.'

Matt waded through the words to reach the only conclusion he could think of. 'She is frightened.'

'In a nutshell, yes.'

Matt blinked several times at the term but decided to leave it for the moment and asked, 'But she has you.'

'A different kind of love. I am her sister, not the male she has chosen to spend her life with. To love and be loved by.'

Clarity made him nod and say, 'Ahh, I see.'

Relieved, Echo stated, 'I hope you do because I know my sister. She will not allow herself to hope that you will want her as much as she needs you.'

Matt asked simply, 'Why?'

'When we lived on Earth, there was only our mother and us.'

'A unit.'

'Yeah, like a squad, I suppose.'

Matt rubbed Shade's ears as he murmured, 'I understand.'

Echo looked doubtfully at him as she asked, 'Do you?'

'Yes, you can rely on your family, trust your family. You believe no one can care for you as much as family will.'

Shocked at how he described her and Relic's feelings about family, the tension eased from her voice. 'Wow, umm... yeah, that is it exactly.'

Hearing the change in her voice, Matt relaxed as well. 'But you are no longer on earth.'

'No... no, we are not, but it is not that simple.' Echo leaned forward as she said, 'Stars, Matt, I wish I could tell you she will be easy, but I cannot. When people look at us, they see me as the fiery, stubborn one.'

'Sharp, honest, blunt.'

Echo laughed. 'Yes, that too. And what do you think they see when they look at Relic?'

Without missing a beat, Matt replied. 'Beauty, resourcefulness, danger, honesty.'

Echo grinned, unoffended he'd left beautiful out when describing her. 'Yes, to all of those. What they miss because she hides it so well is her need to protect those she loves.'

'Explain, please.'

'Again, it is simple. Much of what drives Relic is simple. She will believe, to protect you and Shade, she cannot join her life to yours.'

'Why?'

Shade said thoughtfully. *She thinks if she is killed, we would be lost to our grief and never recover.*

Echo exclaimed, 'Exactly!'

'And she would be right.' Matt held his hand up as Echo went to speak. 'Just as she would grieve if we were to die. But this is no reason to not join our lives together. We must embrace each min while we are alive.'

Softly, Echo agreed, 'Yeah, I would tell her that.'

'So how do I show her how to love me?'

Echo laughed before assuring him. 'Oh, she already loves you. What you need to do is get her to see she does not need to protect you and Shade. Make her see you are there for her, that you need her.'

'And how do you suggest I do that?'

'By telling her how you and Shade were feared, how you both have been rejected because you are different.'

Matt's jaw firmed as his eyes hardened. 'You believe either of us would play on her sympathies in that way? It is dishonest.'

Echo tipped her head to the side and asked, 'Is it because of pride?'

Matt shook his head as Shade grunted in disagreement. 'No, I want a partner, someone who sees us as equals, not people to be pitied.'

Echo said gently, 'Oh, Matt, no one, least of all Relic, could ever pity you two.' She looked at Shade as he stared at her and told him, 'There is nothing to pity and I have no qualms about my sister taking you both as partners. She is lucky you want to include her in your lives. She is not the easiest person to love. In fact, she can be extremely naggy.'

Smiling, Matt asked, 'Naggy, is that a word?'

Echo folded her hands on her desk and stated, 'I stand by the word. Also, she can be bossy and she has a thing about manners.' She looked at the two of them and teasingly asked, 'Are you sure you really want her?'

Matt grinned as Shade told her. *We not only want her, we need her. She completes us.*

Echo sighed softy in relief. 'In that case, there is nothing left to say except Matt and Shade, welcome to our family, as small as it is.'

Matt placed his hand on Shade's head and said, 'We thank you. And Echo, welcome to our family, as small as it is.'

Her expression softened, adding another layer to her, which surprised Matt, and he felt a warm glow ignite in his needar, more so when she said, 'Thank you both.'

Matt gently chided her. 'However, sister, you have not told me how I may win my heart.'

'Ahh, as to that, do you know how to dance?'

'Dance?' asked a bewildered Matt. 'Why do I need to know this?'

Echo grinned at his astonished tone. It was the first time she had heard the Scout Commander be anything but assured. 'Because to win my sister's complete trust, you will have to expose your most vulnerable self.' She looked at Shade as she said. 'The both of you. And to accomplish this, you will need to know how to dance.'

'I do not understand.'

Echo quickly assured him, 'I know you do not, but we have time. I will help you, as will Jax.'

'He will? You have discussed this with him already?'

'I have. Do not be concerned, he will be discreet as he always is.'

Matt nodded, 'I know he will be.'

Echo told him, 'He will provide you with the dance you will perform and I will explain the steps and what they mean when you have watched the vids.'

'Why must this happen?'

'It is a tradition, a custom passed down in our family. There will be two dances. One, I and Relic will perform to say goodbye to our family unit. Then you and Relic will perform your dance, which will symbolize the start of your lives together. Shade will, of course, be included in the dance as well.'

Startled at the admission, Matt asked, 'And this must happen every time a new member is added to the family unit. Even children?'

Echo laughed, then assured him, 'No, no, it's a one-time thing. When and if I ever become mated, I will also have to dance to symbolize my farewell to my family.'

Matt asked, 'Who will you dance with?'

She shrugged away the feeling of melancholy that filled her with his question. The thought of dancing alone broke her heart and again she cursed the people who took her mother from her. Clearing her throat, she tried for a smile and failed. 'I don't know. Forget that for now. I have to tell you part of your dance will be while you are both cloaked.'

Distracted from his thoughts by the unfamiliar word, Matt frowned. 'Cloaked?'

'Oh sorry, that is an old word from Earth. It means hidden or faded.'

I like it. Pronounced Shade. *Cloaked is an excellent description of what we do.*

'Well then, my new friend. I gift you the word. Use it wisely.'

Shade gave her a Prowler grin as he told her. *I like you.*

'As I like you. I have to go. Are you both okay with all of this?'

Matt and Shade both nodded, and then Matt told her, 'If it will give us our future, then yes, we will perform this dance.'

'I thought you would. Good morn, my new brothers. We will talk again soon.'

Matt said goodbye. 'Stay safe, Echo, and protect our heart, until we can.'

Smiling, she nodded, 'That I will.'

Once her image had disappeared, Matt placed his head in his hands. 'Jax, my friend, please show us this dance we must endure -- I am sorry, perform.'

'Certainly Matt. Echo has selected the mating dance.'

'Ah-ahh, why did she not just say it is called the mating dance?'

'It is what I named it, while researching the dance's origins.'

'Is it complicated?'

'Not so much complicated as—'

'As what?'

'Perhaps you and Shade should watch the vid. Then we can discuss your education on terran dancing.'

Echo placed her cup in the recycler and did several complicated dance steps to the door of her cabin. Step one in securing her sister a mate was done. She counted on her fingers, if she was right, there were only two, perhaps three, steps left before Relic was blissfully joined to Matt. She could not wait to see her happy and with someone who loved her. She just hoped she continued on as her Commander, otherwise she may find herself interviewing for a replacement and that would entail speaking and listening to people. A fate worse than death, as far as she was concerned.

EIGHTEEN:

As the first of Otera Majors' four suns rose over the horizon, Relic watched the city come into view from the cruiser. 'Is the port secure?'

Cleo finished her comm, then answered Relic's question, 'Yes, there was no security at any of the docking bays. It appears the Emperor felt it was unnecessary.'

'More fool him,' muttered Echo.

Relic and Cleo smiled, but made no comment. Echo had been in a bad mood ever since Relic told her about Kardan's arrival.

Cleo told her. 'You know it's not our fault, or yours Kardan is coming. It's the Emperor's.'

Echo grumbled as she stared out the window at the docking bay. 'You are right, the one I should be pissed with is that, taje. The Emperor... yeah, he's so toast.'

When the signal came for them to disembark, Glenn asked Cleo, 'Does that mean the Emperor is in trouble?'

Cleo grinned and whispered in reply, 'He has no idea what trouble comes his way and Glenn, my friend, remember to keep your head down when the missiles start.'

'She is to shoot the Emperor?!'

With a twinkle in her eye, she nodded. 'If he's lucky.' With that, Cleo started issuing her orders. 'My units to me,' then she marched from the cruiser as her Warriors filed from the ship.

When Charis came even with Glenn, she asked, 'Learn anything new?'

'I did. I believe I was just warned to stay out of the Negotiator's way.'

Charis slapped his shoulder. 'See, every day you understand us better.'

Glen grimaced as he moaned, 'And the more I learn, the less I know.'

Relic told him when she came up behind him, 'Only a wise male knows that.'

'Then I must be the wisest of males.'

Relic grinned. 'Nah, but you are getting there.'

They all had time to look around as they made their slow way from the port to the presidential palace. Relic watched Cleo instruct her people using sign language, which all the Armee were using now, thanks to Kardan. He had become enamored of the language when he had seen several versions of it on a vid. At his urging, Peyton and Trina had found instructors to create their own sign language and then teach it to the Warriors and Scouts.

Relic said as she looked up at a newly constructed high-rise, 'This reminds me of New York.'

Echo looked around as the walkway moved them along. 'Old New York or new New York?'

'The new one.'

Cleo murmured, 'I never made it there.'

'Neither did I,' Charis stated. 'I was too busy down south.'

Cleo asked her, 'Were you one of Netta's back then?'

Charis smiled. 'Yes, me and a few others.'

Echo praised her, 'Nice work.'

Startled, Charis asked, 'Oh, you knew about us?'

'Oh sure, the organization Relic and I ran with knew just about everyone who was making noise.'

Charis chided her, 'Yeah right, they didn't know about Peyton.'

Echo shrugged, 'Well no, but seriously she had Darby.'

'I'll give you that.'

Cleo asked with a laugh, 'And who in their right mind would willingly go up against Darby?'

They all chorused, 'No one we know!'

'That is what I am saying.'

At a signal from one of her Warriors, Cleo abruptly stated, 'This is where I leave you. Please stay safe and remember, I and my people are only a comm away.'

Relic nodded, 'We will. Stay safe too. We need you.'

Cleo grinned. 'Oh, I know,' then she stepped off the walkway to join several Warriors waiting for her. Relic was sure she spotted Mayton in the group. Echo said as she watched her and her Warriors turn a corner, 'I like her.'

Relic returned, 'As do I.'

Echo muttered, 'I hope she stays with us.'

Relic grinned, 'As do I.'

NINETEEN:

Ten minutes later, Echo and her people walked into the presidential residence of Emperor Alinac Zesiro. Relic sniggered when she saw the decor, which was once again red and gold. 'I am thinking it's their colors.'

Echo sighed and shook her head. 'Honestly, when will they learn red and gold can be overdone, and it leaves much to be desired?'

Charis muttered, 'I think they should be struck from the color pallet.'

Glenn asked, 'Can you do that?'

Charis hummed, then said, 'I could ask the Star Daughter to do it.'

Relic grinned and told her, 'If she won't get rid of pink for Darby and Netta, there is not a chance in hayda she'll get rid of gold or red for you.'

Charis sighed loudly, 'You are probably right, but it could be worth a shot.'

'Could be,' stated Echo. 'Ah-ha, it looks as though we have arrived at the Emperor's throne room. How enchanting.'

Relic smirked as they came to a halt several feet from large golden doors and asked, 'What gave it away? Is it the enormous doors or the two giant guardsmen standing barring our way?'

Echo laughed, 'Guess!'

With a sweep of her hand, Relic said, 'Never mind, Charis, Glenn, if you would, please?'

At her command, both Captains rushed forward and disabled the guards before they had time to realize what was happening.

'Excellent technique,' Echo murmured as she watched several warriors hurry forward to gag and cuff the males. 'That looked suspiciously like the Esmond technique.'

Relic agreed, 'It was. Esmond taught it to me himself a few years back, and I taught it to my guard's last weken. How do you know it?'

'Simone, his daughter, showed it to me when I was on a mission with her.'

'Huh, that must have been interesting.'

'Oh, it was.'

'You think they are alright?'

Echo looked over at her sister and her own expression softened when she saw the worry on her face. 'I hope they are, but if you want, we can try to find out.'

'Yeah, I'd like that.'

'So we will.'

As Echo and Relic waited for the males to be dragged from in front of the doors, Relic praised both Captains. 'Well done, both of you. Are they still breathing?'

'They are.' Charis looked at Glenn, 'Well, mine is.'

He raised a sardonic eyebrow as he replied to the unasked question, 'As is mine. That is, after all, the reason for the punch and hold. Is it not?'

Relic nodded. 'It is, and you performed it with professionalism, which we both appreciate, do we not, Negotiator?'

Echo agreed wholeheartedly, 'Oh, definitely. Now, should we enter the lion's den and find out who awaits us?'

Relic whispered as they waited for her guards to form a defensive ring around Echo, 'You are enjoying this way too much.'

'Aww, now you sound just like Darby.'

'With reason,' Relic snapped as the doors were suddenly pulled open by armed guards. Instantly Echo's guards swarmed them and within a blink of an eye the seven large males were subdued, cuffed and gagged.

Echo entered the room with Relic and Glenn on either side of her. The throne room was as opulent as she had expected it to be. Again, the decorator had relied heavily on the colors red and gold. The only relief from the oppressive atmosphere was one entire wall made from glass, which overlooked the city below. Once they reached the middle of the room, they stopped and looked up at the male sitting on a golden throne. He was flanked on either side by a tall male and a short, squat, scaly green male.

As Echo made to step forward, Glenn placed an arm in her way, preventing her from taking a step forward. Relic asked softly in German, which she knew Glenn had studied extensively, 'Why have we stopped?'

Without removing his eyes from the green male, Glenn replied, also in German, 'He is a Lermon, a secretive species, seldom seen off their world.'

The male squirmed and gurgled something on hearing the word Lermon to the other two males. Which made them both stare hard at Glenn. Echo asked, 'Is he dangerous?'

'Yes. Their only weapon is a venom, which is secreted from their fingertips. They wipe the venom on their tongue and make a ball, then spit it at their enemies. It has been reported they are used exclusively by Raiders. There is no known cure against their venom, at least,' he corrected himself, 'that I know of. Commander Harm may know of one or Lord Klune. Anyone who is unlucky enough to come in contact with their venom dies an excruciating painful death.'

Echo asked quietly, 'You have witnessed this?'

'Yes, when I ran with the Raiders, many yentas ago.'

Relic murmured, still in German. 'You, my friend, have lived an interesting life.'

'I have in more ways than one,' was his only comment.

Echo asked as she eyed the green male who she thought looked exceedingly nervous, although the Emperor and his brother remained relaxed, which annoyed her, 'What about Warriors? Can his venom kill you?'

Glenn's face tightened in remembered pain as he replied, 'No, we are only left disfigured.'

Echo's eyes hardened at the answer, 'Can they be killed?'

'Yes.'

'Options Commander?'

Relic quickly asked, 'Statement or threat?'

'Both.'

'Then I suggest we remove the threat and make a statement. Glenn, where is his heart?'

'Stomach, to the left above his groin.'

'Skin's composition?'

'Soft, much like terrans.'

Relic reached into her pocket, took out a small blowpipe, and before the Emperor or the two males realized what she was about to do, she blew two darts toward the green male, hitting him in his lower abdomen. The male cried out only once before toppling down the steps to lie still on the tiled floor. The Emperor's brother rushed to the male and put his hand on his forehead. After a minute, he glanced up at the Emperor, who had stood up and shook his head. Echo whispered to Glenn, 'Have the body removed to the Intercessor and ask Avery to comm Lord Klune and ask him how she should preserve it. Please stress how toxic the male is please.'

'As you will, Negotiator.'

Emperor Zesiro, was a handsome male, and was said to be 150 yentas old. He had warrior-short black hair and bore a striking resemblance to his son, except his features were more mature. Echo observed that if his son lived to be as old as his father, he would have many of the same qualities that she saw in the male who was gazing at her. However, he would lack the glint of cruelty simmering in Alinac's amber eyes and the physique honed by years of training that was concealed beneath the fine clothing he donned.

Alinac knew as he looked at the invaders standing in his throne room, he may never see another sunrise. With that in mind, he asked, 'Why kill him?'

Echo shrugged and returned, 'Why allow him here?' She walked closer to the steps and ordered. 'Come down off your throne and we will have a discussion. You, Emperor Alinac Zesiro, have been invaded and, for a former Raider, I am sure you understand the implications of that.'

Alinac stepped down to join his brother, as he asked, 'You think I was a Raider? You are sorely misguided.'

Echo grinned. 'I see what you are attempting to do there. If it makes you feel better to protest a fact, then do so, but know this. I know the truth of how and why you are here, as do the Star Daughter and her mate, who will arrive within hours.'

Relic smirked as she stated, 'You see how he has not protested the mention of the Star Daughter?'

'You're right Commander. So, what say you Emperor, is my Commander right? Do you know of the emergence of the Star Daughter?'

Alinac felt the urge to squirm, just as he had done in his youth, but his many years of practicing self-control prevented him from showing any visible reaction to the mention of the Star Daughter. Stiffly, he responded to Echo's taunts. 'I, as with all worlds, witnessed the grand meeting and the Star Daughter's performance.'

'Oh, she is not going to like that term.' Echo looked at the male and said seriously, 'I would advise you not to use it again. It will only get you dead.'

'As if I am not already dead.'

Echo shrugged. 'That is to be determined. For now, we are to have a conversation.'

'About what?'

'About you making it impossible for the citizens of Otera Major to remain here.'

Alinac glanced at his brother Baen and shook his head when he saw him formulating a reply. 'Those are spurious accusations.'

'Spurious indeed!' Echo smiled. 'Well, we shall see Emperor, we shall see. 'But I digress. Where should we have our discussion? Commander, any suggestions?'

Relic flicked her eyes towards the brothers as she answered, 'Captain Charis has found what she thinks is a conference room.'

'Is it acceptable to you?'

'Yes, it is being secured now.'

'Okay.'

Relic made several signs to her Warriors, then said, 'Follow me, please.'

With any protests the brothers walked toward the open doors, Echo followed the two brothers and asked Glenn who walked next to her, 'Captain Glenn, can you please supervise the prisoners' transfer from the Battlecruiser? I think it is time they joined us in the conference room.'

'As you will, Negotiator.'

'Oh, and have coffee sent down, please. I feel I will need fortifying.'

With a grin barely hidden, Glenn once more stated, 'As you will, Negotiator.'

Echo was sure she heard Relic mutter the word addict, but did not call her on it because her attention was taken by several Warriors surrounding the Emperor and his brother to search and scan them both.

Echo was happy to find that the conference room had a nice cream and brown color scheme. Once the brothers were seated, Relic stationed her guards around the room before taking her seat next to Echo and starting to read from her tablet. 'Commander Cleo has secured the city. Captain Mayton has contacted the informer and they have transported her and her family to the Intercessor.'

'Are they well?'

'Yes. Mayton and his scouts have joined up with Cleo's Warriors. She and her units have secured the city, and she is now coordinating the planetwide lockdown.'

Echo drummed her fingers on the table as she stared at the opposite wall. 'Alright. When it is safe, have Avery set up a medical center and have Chef Enid and her chefs provide food if it's needed. Tell her I said meat is to be supplied, not just vegetables.'

'Will do.'

Echo looked at the door as it was thrust open to reveal

Ziv who was carrying a tray and behind him was Judge, also carrying a tray. Echo hissed with displeasure. 'What the hayda!?'

Ziv scolded. 'Such language and from the Negotiator, you should be setting an example.'

Echo snapped, 'Seriously!'

They both placed their trays on the table and as Echo pulled the coffee urn toward her, Ziv said, 'You will need us both.'

'Is that right?'

'Yes. In case you forgot, I am a Mystic and protocol dictates, I should have already been invited.' He frowned at Echo, who Relic saw had the decency to blush at the reprimand.

Judge crossed his arms and stated, 'I am here because I was a prisoner and I will know when they lie, which we all know they will. Is that not right, Emperor?'

Baen snarled, 'Watch your tongue, one arm.'

'Was that meant to be a slur?' asked Relic, 'because if it was, it was just stupid.'

Judge laughed as Echo shook her head. 'That was just sad.' Then all humor fled as she told the male, 'Speak again like that to any of my people and I will not only slit your throat. I will place your head at the entrance to the Empirer so all can see what happens to royalty who do not mind their manners. Do I make myself clear?'

'How dare—'

Alinac placed his hand on his brother's quivering arm as he told him, 'Baen, enough.' He addressed Echo. 'We understand and apologize for the untoward slur.'

Mockingly, Relic murmured loud enough for all to hear, 'So polite.'

In the same tone, Echo agreed. 'Isn't he, though?' She nodded to Judge to take a seat as she told the two newcomers, 'We are waiting for the prisoners to arrive.'

TWENTY:

One cup of coffee later, the door reopened, and the prisoners were escorted in. 'Still naked, I see,' Echo murmured and was unable to hold back her grin, even more so when she heard Ziv and Judge's gasps of surprise.

Relic shrugged, 'Yep.'

'What is the meaning of this?' demanded the outraged Emperor.

'Your daughter refused to dress.' Echo spread her hands as she asked with a glint of humor in her eyes for all to see, 'What would you have me do?'

She waited for his response, but he was too busy taking off his jacket and draping it over his daughter, while his brother greeted their sister. Echo murmured to Relic, 'Probably should let her dress.'

Relic pursed her lips as she pondered the situation, 'You think?'

Echo shrugged this time, 'Yep, get her some clothes. Her naked ass is making me want to throw up my coffee, which would be a shame. It is really good coffee.'

Relic supplied, 'Peyton's special brand.'

Glancing at her sister, Echo motioned for Charis to find clothes for the naked female before turning to her and asking, "Did you steal it?"

Relic looked at her sister as both Ziv and Judge smothered laughs. 'Oh, my stars. No! Why would you even think that?'

'Just wondered. So how did we get it?'

Relic's eyes narrowed as she asked her, 'Why do you sound disappointed?'

'I don't, not really… its good you didn't. I think Peyton would not be so forgiving. I mean, it is her coffee, right?'

Locking her lips against all the things she wanted to say, Relic hissed, 'Lady Esther stocked the dispensers. She said we would need proper coffee.'

Echo sighed, 'She wasn't wrong.'

This time it was Relic who drummed her fingers on the table and asked in English, 'This is not going to end well, is it?'

'No, it's gone too far now.'

'How did you know he was a Raider?'

Echo shrugged. 'If you think about it, you'll see why I came to that conclusion. Oh, and while I am at it, can you have Kido and Haruto come on down? We need everything from their comps.'

Relic murmured, 'As you will.'

Echo struggled to suppress a laugh as Jillana pitifully complained to her father and uncle, throwing hateful glares their way. To make matters worse, Jillana made a big fuss about getting dressed, which had Echo clenching her teeth in frustration. Finally, Relic motioned for Charis to push the female into a chair before Echo made good on the threat simmering in her eyes.

Charis grabbed the female's shoulders and frog marched her backward to a chair and forced her to sit. Then she placed her mouth against Jillana's ear as she easily held her in place and whispered, 'Think before you decide to continue on making a spectacle of yourself and look at the Negotiators face. She is about ready to have you removed from the room.' Jillana looked up at the Warrior ready to dismiss her and her warning with blistering sarcasm when Charis smiled coldly and said, 'And by remove, I mean have you dragged from here and killed.'

With that, Charis walked back to her position by the door. Jillana's father quietly told his daughter, 'Jillana, take heed of the warning. We are at the mercy of a female who knows too much about us. Give her no excuse to slaughter us.'

Jillana cowered in her seat as her father's warning followed close on the heels of the Warriors. She glanced at Echo, who fixed her with an unflinching stare, her face giving nothing away. The absence of any discernible emotion was even more chilling than the threat of punishment. Jillana silently closed the clasps on her dress as she whispered, 'Yes, father.'

When the room fell silent once more, Echo smiled thinly and stated, 'This is how this meeting is going to go. I will ask questions; you will give me answers. For every untruth told by any of you. I will have one person removed from the room and imprisoned where you will be subjected to drugs and any number of ugly things. The choice will be yours.'

'You lie! You will not hurt us,' snarled Lady Gittar.

Echo's smile disappeared as she leaned back in her chair and stated, 'Oh, but I will, Lady Gittar, you belong to me now and are playing my game. Ask your brother if I lie.'

Gittar fearfully turned to her brother and asked tearfully, 'Alinac, is what she says true?'

Without removing his eyes from Echo, the Emperor pleaded, 'Gittar remain silent. I beg of you, do not argue.'

'But—'

Baen pleaded, 'Sister, please.'

When they were quiet, Echo continued. 'So easy question, first. Who organizes the tornays?'

Baen and Alinac raised their hands. She looked to Judge for confirmation, with a silent nod he agreed. 'And who recruits the fighters?'

Baen's hand remained in the air. Again, Judge nodded. 'Okay, now whose idea was it to remove all the citizens from the world?' No one raised a hand. 'Come on, it had to be someone's.'

Alinac said in a low voice, 'You are assuming your information is correct.'

'I don't assume anything; I know it is correct. But let's set that aside for now, it is not relevant anymore since it will not happen. Instead, I am curious as to why you chose this world to retire on. The planet was dying, so what drew you here?'

Alinac made himself comfortable or as comfortable as he could under the circumstances and prepared to answer her. But before he could speak, his son interrupted and asked Echo, 'I would like to know what species you are.'

'Why?'

'Curiosity.'

Relic grinned and asked Echo, 'Does he truly think you will tell him where we come from so he can get fighters or send his father's friends to our world?'

'I'm thinking both ideas have crossed his mind. You know that old saying, Commander Relic? Once a Raider, always a Raider.'

Alinac watched the females and silently applauded his son. Of course, this was simple. What had put him off his game was their sudden appearance and the death of Sakal. It had been many yentas since he played this game. He now realized where his son was leading him and stated, 'My son is not wrong. Your species would be a novelty. There is an opportunity here for us all, if we could obtain females like your Commander and female warriors. We could hold the first female tornays. We would make more credits than you have ever seen. Is that not right, Baen?'

Baen nodded his head frantically, realizing his brother and nephew's strategy. Alinac had repeatedly told him that everyone had a price, and it seemed they had discovered this female's price. With a smile, Baen agreed, 'No other world could compete with us. We would be the first, holding exclusive contracts. You and your kind would be revered as goddesses among the fighters.'

Echo looked firstly at Relic who smirked, then at Ziv who just closed his eyes in despair.

Judge raised his eyebrow as he told her. 'They live by the creed. Everyone has a price.'

Echo nodded then sipped her cooling coffee before saying, 'No, we are not for sale, nor is our homeworld.'

Alinac smirked as he crossed his arms, 'Are you so sure you are correct?'

'Yes, the Star Daughter would not be pleased. So, no.'

Baen smirked as he tried cajoling her. 'Really, I think you protest too much. There is always a way to find an agreement. You just have to be willing to look for it.'

Echo sighed and beat a quick tattoo on the table then asked, 'Alinac, do you seriously think you are getting out of this?' She scanned the faces of his family and asked, 'That any of you are? The Amahka called a howl and has placed a priounty for information and the capture of any Raider. I figure by the time he and the Kail have discovered every bit of information contained within your minds, there won't be much left of you.'

Alinac scoffed at the notion of a howl being sounded. 'A howl, do you know what that is?'

Echo softly told him, 'Yes, sadly I do. Do you, because your words say you do not.'

'It is a myth, a legend told to frighten new Raiders.'

Echo shook her head, 'Just as the Star Daughter was supposedly a myth. Look how untrue that was.'

Alinac took a deep breath before ridiculing her statement. 'You are trying to scare us with your threats, but let me tell you, better people than you have tried and failed.'

Echo stared at him for a full minute deciding if the male was stupid or just blind to his situation, finally she said, 'I am sure they have. So, as you are not going to play nicely and I am tired of staring at you, I call this meeting over. Commander, have them sent to the cells to await the Amahka.'

'As you will, Negotiator.'

Echo stood and as she made for the doors, ordered, 'Captain Glenn and Charis with me.'

TWENTY-ONE:

Dillon woke just as someone entered his cell. His senses, those his abductors had left him, told him the person was female. He silently groaned when he caught her scent. She smelled of the sands of Casdam, hard with an under-taste of the sweet fruit buried within the caves, enticing but deadly.

He thought they were done using females to entice him to bed them, after they realize he could not perform intercourse. Perhaps, she was sent by the devlish himself to add another layer of pain to his already aching body. Grimly, he wondered what new torture they had devised to break him and bend him to their will, to turn him into an unfeeling, uncaring killer. Nothing he'd endured so far had induced him to kill his opponents. Even holding his brothers from him had not worked. For now, he remained unbroken, but every day it was becoming harder and harder to remember why he resisted.

With his eyes shut and his breathing steady, he focused his senses to explore the surrounding area. He detected the presence of three individuals standing beyond the cell doors. Was this the opportunity he had been waiting for to compel his captors to free him, or was it just another one of the furiners' experiments to assess his compliance? Despite the uncertainty, Dillion realized that he had to take advantage of this slim chance of success. His heart almost stopped when he heard a female demand harshly, 'Echo, what are you doing?'

Echo turned to her sister and cursed. She had been sure Relic was busy in the cells next door.

'Relic, he's drugged. I need to see if he is okay.'

'Who told you he was drugged?'

Echo nodded her head at the blue male in a red lab coat standing between Glenn and Charis. 'He did. He says he's the chief medical officer for the Emperor.'

Relic moved to stand in front of the tall, thin, balding male and snarled, 'Is he drugged or did you lie? Because if anything happens to her, I will kill you where you stand.'

The male gulped audibly and sweat broke out on his face as he stared into eyes that promised death. 'No, no, this is a drug of my own making. It renders him compliant and allows us to direct him.'

Relic watched the male for several seconds longer and then told him, 'Let us hope you are correct.' She then flicked her comm unit on. 'Avery, you and Haruto need to come to the cells. I need you to oversee the download of the contents of—'

'Sinkko, Prr—'

"I don't care!' snapped Relic, her eyes fixed on the male daring him to speak again. She then told Avery, 'Some healer claims to have developed a drug that will make our Elite more compliant.'

She heard Avery snort and then say, 'That sounds like bull. We are on our way.'

Relic turned back in time to see the Elite rise from the bed and wrap one hard arm around Echo's midriff and place his other hand around her throat. Wild eyes stared at Relic as she took a step toward the cell door. He shook his head and a rusty voice ordered, 'Do not, or she dies. Ripping her throat from her body would give me no pleasure, but I will do it.'

'I believe you,' Relic told him as she eased back on her heels. 'I understand why you are annoyed. Sneaking up on a male when he is pretending to sleep is a nutoro move and something I have told her not to do, but—' She shrugged, 'younger sisters just never listen.'

Dillion felt the female in his arms sigh and murmur something. He relaxed his hold on her waist and pushed her back against the wall, keeping his hand on her throat. He looked down at her, asking, 'What did you say?'

'I said older sisters are so dayam annoying when they are right.'

Dillion raised an eyebrow as he said, 'You should listen to

your sister. She obviously understands Warriors.'

'Well yeah, sure, take her side.'

'There are no sides, only common—' Dillion caught himself as he began to argue with the female and growled, 'What are you, female?'

Echo made the sign for calm as she saw movement from the corner of her eye. Gently, she told him, 'I am the Negotiator for the Star Daughter.'

'Star Daughter, so I was right.' he murmured 'She has emerged.'

'Yes, and has established a home for you and—'

'Silence!' he demanded. 'How do I know what you say is true?'

Echo grimaced as Relic asked, 'Oh good point, I suppose telling you we do not lie will not reassure you?'

The hand on Echo's throat tightened again as he looked over his shoulder at her, 'No, I have been tricked too often to fall for pretty words.'

Relic refused to panic as she watched Echo struggle for air. She quickly made the sign to Glenn and Charis to stand down as their hands moved to their blasters. Her voice was calm but her heart raced as she asked the giant Warrior.

'Yeah, umm, can you let my sister breathe? She's turning red, which, for our species, means she is dying.'

Dillion instantly relaxed his hold and Echo drew in air as she wheezed. 'Thanks for letting go.' Her eyes widened when she looked past Relic and saw Kardan and Jarrod emerge from the lift. 'Oh tuap, that's not good.' She quickly whispered to the male. 'Listen, I know you do not trust us or me, but you have to release me and make it fast.'

'No, you are the only thing keeping the male from drugging me again.'

With another look to see how far Kardan was from her. She shook her head. 'No, I vow no one will drug you.'

'Your words mean nothing to me.'

'Look handsome, that male coming here is Kardan Roeah. You know who that is, right?'

Dillion's eyes narrowed, but he refused to look behind him, keeping his eyes on the female in his hold. 'He is dead, as are his brothers.'

'No, he is alive, just as they are.'

Dillion snarled, 'Now I know you lie. Wolf is lost and Kardan and Reeve are dead.'

Curious to hear what his answer would be, she asked, 'What of Hawk?'

Dillion shook his head as his eyes clouded over. 'He… he is… I do not know. Stop trying to trick me.'

'I vow I am not. What I am telling you is true. Kardan is mated to the Star Daughter. He was elevated by the Star Child to Amahka Elite Kardan. And the male with him is the Kail. You know who that is, right?'

'That is impossible.'

A voice that shook Dillion's needar asked gently, 'Why should that be impossible? Many things we thought were not possible as youths are now possible, just as your survival is possible.'

Dillion's eyes pleaded with Echo to swear that what he heard was true and not a dream. Smiling gently, she nodded. 'I know you don't believe me, but believe what your senses tell you. He is Kardan, this it is not a dream.'

His hand fell away from her throat, 'I cannot—'

Echo placed her hand on his trembling arm. 'I understand your hesitation. It is hard to accept freedom after being reduced to a drug-induced reality, but Kardan is here to prove you are free now. Turn and see for yourself.'

Dillion's voice was a mere whisper as he said, 'I am unworthy.'

Echo's voice was gentle as she whispered, 'I know. I felt the same when I met the Star Daughter for the first time. So now I strive to prove her faith in me is not wasted as I know you will.'

With a nod, Dillion squared his shoulders and turned to stare at a male he believed gone from his world. 'I never broke. I came close, but I remained an Elite.'

Kardan allowed Echo to slip from the cell. He would speak with her later. For now, his attention was on the Elite standing before him. 'I believe you. I am more than proud of the strength and courage you have shown in your battle to remain sane, and to hold to the values of the Star Daughter's Elites.'

Dillion nodded once only then asked, 'My brothers?'

Glenn stepped forward, 'They are safe. We have recovered them from the cells beneath these.'

Again, Dillion nodded once. Kardan asked him, 'Can you walk?'

'I wish to say yes, but I fear the drugs they fed me have sapped any ability I have to do more than I am doing.'

Jarrod asked, 'So what was your plan?'

Dillion's laugh was rusty as he returned, 'What plan?'

'I like him,' stated Echo from outside the cell.

Kardan half turned as he asked, 'Are you still here, Negotiator?'

'Umm no, I'm like the wind and gone.'

Relic growled, 'Why are you not moving?'

Echo stalled, 'I don't want him to be alone.'

Jarrod assured her, 'He will not be. I will remain with him.'

'Okay, well see you… umm, what are you called?'

'Dillion, my name is Dillion Caste.'

'Great name. Okay then. See you sometime, Dillion Caste.' With that, Echo ran from the room with Relic and Charis walking slowly after her.

Dillion watched them go, then stated, 'She is different.'

Kardan agreed, 'She is unique, ahh, here is our healer. Dinas, are you here to assist our Elite Dillion?'

Dinas smiled, 'I am. Elite Dillion, allow me to escort you to our Warship where I will remove the drugs from your system so you can heal.'

'Thank you, Elite Dinas. I am pleased you remain alive.'

'As is my mate.' When Dillion opened his mouth to ask questions, Dinas told him. 'Yes, I have a mate and yes, I can perform the act of intercourse. You will also be able to do so with your mate. For now, allow me to heal you and then I will explain how all this is possible.'

As they helped Dillion onto a floater, Jarrod smirked and murmured to Kardan, 'He is showing off because he was first in his sex-ed class.'

Kardan hid his smile as he inclined his head, 'I have heard that from many Warriors.'

'Probably everyone he has told. Not that he brags or anything,' Jarrod assured him with a smile.

Kardan pulled on his bottom lip as he'd seen Jarrod's father do, and now understood the reason for it. It helped to keep the laughter from escaping, 'No, of course not, why would he have to.'

Dinas snarled, 'You know you two are not as funny as you think you are.'

Jarrod shrugged, 'But we have been practicing.'

'Save me!' muttered Dinas as he moved the floating bed from the cell.

Dillion craned his head around to take one last look at the cells. That was when the fear grabbed his heart and he grasped Dinas's arm.

'Am I truly free?'

'Yes, my friend, you are. With Kail Jarrod's help, you will put the past behind you where it should be and look toward a future that is of your own choosing.'

As his hand dropped away, Dillion's eyes were caught and held by Kardan's. In them he saw a timeless faith for him and in him.

'Alright… alright.'

TWENTY-TWO:

Later that night when Judge fell into bed on board Prowler II, he ran over all that he had been through that day, meeting the Amahka, spending a few mins with Dillion before he was placed in the regen, talking with the Kail, who he was pleased to discover still had his dry sense of humor.

Jarrod assured him the feeling of being overwhelmed was because of the recent changes in his life and the feeling would dissipate when he found his purpose in life. What kept him awake now was the thought of having to say goodbye to Echo and Relic tomorrow. He lay with his hands under his head as he sorted through his feelings and discovered it was not just leaving Echo and Relic behind that had him concerned. He did not want to leave the world or the people he had come to know. 'Jax, may I speak with you?'

'Yes, Captain Shaw.'

'Please, call me Judge.'

'I thank you, Judge. What can I help you with?'

'When we leave this world. Do you leave as well?'

'No, I am able to stay for as long as the Star Daughter wishes me to.'

'I see.' As he turned over and thumped his pillow, he said, 'Thank you. I feel comforted with the knowledge our people will not be alone and unguarded.'

'I will endeavor to keep them safe.'

'Thanks, Jax.'

'It was a pleasure talking to you, Judge.'

As Judge drifted into sleep, he murmured, 'You will make a good friend.'

Jax silently agreed he would.

Judge looked around and smiled when he saw the female

standing by a gate. 'Greetings, Star Daughter.'

'Greetings. Oh, you know who I am.'

'I do, and I know this is your home where you were raised.'

Peyton smiled. 'Yes, it was. I was loved here.'

'I can see that. It shines in every part of your construct.'

Peyton opened the gate and swept her hand out, 'Please enter and join me on the porch.'

Judge walked through the gate and up to the house. He waited until she had taken her seat before sitting on the rocking chair. 'This is peaceful.'

Peyton nodded in agreement. 'I try to keep it that way. It's my escape place, somewhere I go to when things become overwhelming.'

'Once I would have said it would be impossible to think of the Star Daughter needing a sanctuary. But recently I discovered all species can become overwhelmed and need somewhere to find their balance again.'

'You have spoken to Jarrod, haven't you?'

Judge nodded. 'I have done so. I always found him to be an extremely intelligent and complicated male with a sound sense of humor.'

Peyton looked over at him and said, 'It sounds as if you have met him before.'

'We did, several times in the past in very different situations. He and I were both different males then.'

'Time changes everything.'

Judge agreed, then said, 'Or the emergence of an unusual Star Daughter does.'

'Perhaps.'

Judge smiled at her non-committal agreement. 'Why am I here again?'

'You are well?'

'Yes.' He flexed his arm and fingers. 'Yes, extremely well.'

'You look healthier than you did last time you were here.'

'Thank you. I am recovering faster than the healer thought I would.' He looked at her and asked. 'Would that be at your will?'

She smiled and began to rock. 'Perhaps. Are you happy Judge Shaw?'

He took a deep breath in and then let it out before saying. 'No, I am not. Please do not think I am ungrateful for everything that has changed in my life. I am more than grateful but happy, no.'

'Why?'

'I will miss Echo and Relic when I return to Maikonia.'

'You do realize they will not stay on Otera Major. They will also return home.'

'I know, and I wish to see our home, to discover old friends and make new ones. Although I find I am apprehensive about remaining there permanently.'

'What do you wish to do?'

'Something that needs doing. I am not willing to sit around or retrain in another profession. I am a Warrior of justice. It was what they created me for.'

Peyton rocked quietly for a moment before saying, 'Yes, you were. There were not many like you created. You are unique among Warriors.'

Judge shook his head. 'I am sad to hear that. I had hoped they had created more of my kind.'

Peyton smiled slowly. 'They may have but if so, we have not found them yet.'

'Is it likely they will be found?'

Peyton shrugged, 'Don't give up hope, it is early days still.'

'What does that mean?'

'It means not every Warrior has been released from stasis and we are still finding Warriors like you and the others rescued here. So, there is hope we will find more Justice Warriors.'

'I did not know that. So until then, what can I do?'

'As to that, I have a mission for you. Remember, you may say no if you want to, but know this. If you accept, this will not be a permanent position unless you wish it to be so.'

Judge inclined his head in acknowledgement. 'What, Madam, is this position?'

'I want you to take over the ruling of Major Otera.'

Judge stared at her for several minutes, not blinking or moving. Finally, he asked, 'Can you repeat that, please?' She did, then waited for his reply. 'Why would you think I would want to do this?'

'Because you are the right person for this position. You know how the fighters should be treated. How they should be managed. You can and will enforce the rules by teaching other people to referee with discipline and ethics. This world needs the tornays, whether or not we like it. They keep the world alive. You, Judge Shaw, would make it so the people who live here are valued and employed.'

Scratching his cheek, he asked, 'How?'

'By training them in the care and housing of fighters. You will show them the correct way to keep the fighters healthy with exercise and nourishing meals. You will recognize when a fighter is in trouble and train others to understand what signs to look for and when they need to call in advocates for the fighters. I will send traders, healers, and instructors to help with rebuilding this world. You, Judge, can make this world as unique as you are, and to do that, you will use what is already established. Except you will stamp out the corruption and turn the tornays into an ethical business.'

Judge rubbed his cheek again as he said, 'I would have to build the arenas that are already planned, as well as the high-rises for housing fighters and their managers. We could build Hutells and staff them with residents.'

'Yes, and yes to all that.'

A gleam entered Judge's eyes. 'I can do this.'

'Yes, you can.'

'But I will not want to be locked here forever.'

Peyton nodded as she rocked. 'As I said, when you decide you have done all you want to, you can select your replacement.'

'What would my title be?'

Peyton scrunched her nose up as she asked, 'Do you need one?'

Judge grinned at her tone. 'Titles and designations, are

essential to ruling. At least that is what I have observed in the Tornay worlds I have been to. It has to do with building respect.'

'Huh, never looked at it like that. So what do you want to be called?'

Judge thought for a minute as he set his chair to rocking, then a slow smile spread over his face. 'Governor.'

Peyton smiled as well. 'Governor Judge Shaw. Yeah, it has a nice authoritative ring to it.'

'Alright, I will do it, but my first order will be to change the name of the world.'

'Oh well, if the people agree, then do so.'

Judge smiled, recognizing the tone in her voice. 'Did you have any names in mind? If the people agree, that is.'

'Well now, you have mentioned it, yes... yes, I do.'

'Pray tell, what is it?'

With a grin, she told him. 'Kelara.'

Frowning at the unusual name, he asked. 'And what does Kelara mean?'

'It is an old language from a world long forgotten. It means champion or great fighter.'

Judge repeated the name silently to himself a few times and then nodded. 'It is a worthy name for a world that will hold the most legal competitive tornays owned and blessed by the Star Daughter.'

'Under your leadership.'

'If it pleases you, Madam, then yes.'

'Good, now you get to explain it to Echo and Relic.'

Judge opened his mouth, but no words escaped and then he was back in his bed alone.

'Dayam it!' he grumbled as he turned over 'They are not going to like this. Not at all.'

Peyton whispered, *I know that is why you are telling them.*

TWENTY-THREE:

Shortly after Dillion had been transported to Prowler II, Echo found herself having an uncomfortable conversation with Kardan about the needless risk she had taken for herself and her Warriors. She felt thoroughly chastised and later told Relic during a late-night snack that it was like being scolded by their mother. Relic had been completely unsympathetic, until Echo promised never to do something like that again.

Now it was the following night and Kardan was leaving with the Emperor, his family and the rescued fighters, Judge included. Echo knew she was going to miss him because what she had planned for the world was going to take someone like Judge to oversee it. As she gazed out into space, she admitted she was hiding; she did not want Judge or, if she was honest with herself, Kardan to leave. Feeling vulnerable was a new emotion for her, and not one she particularly enjoyed.

When the door opened, she was surprised to see Kardan striding into the conference room. He smiled as he pulled a chair out at the end of the table and sat. Echo's heart did a slow roll as she muttered, 'I thought you had left.'

'My departure is imminent. But I have time to listen to your proposal.'

'How do you know I have one?'

With a smile once again playing on his lips, he raised a dark eyebrow and asked, 'Do you not?'

With a grimace, she admitted, 'Yeah, I do.'

She slid the tablet over to him and then stood and walked around the room as he read her plans. He nodded a few times, then closed the tablet. Echo retook her seat and asked, 'So what do you think?'

Kardan smiled. 'I think I have no opinion. This is your

mission and your decision.'

'Tuap, not even a hint?'

Standing, Kardan shook his head. 'I bid you goodbye, and know I have faith in your judgment.'

Scowling, Echo stood as well. 'You know that is just an evasion, right?'

Smiling fully as he walked to the door, he told her, 'So I have been told. I will see you when you return.'

Not wanting to watch him go and admit she was feeling vulnerable again, she stared out the window into the blackness of space and muttered, 'Whatever.'

Stopping in the doorway, Kardan looked back at the small female. 'Echo.'

Echo refocused on him, 'Yes.'

'We have faith in you, have faith in yourself to know what is right for the people of this world.'

Echo's anxiety melted away at his words. 'Thank you, Kardan. That means a lot.'

'As I hoped it would.' The door slid silently closed behind him.

Falling back into her chair, she mumbled, 'But still not helpful.'

She remained where she was for another hour, and turned over all the possibilities she could think of finally concluding there was no way for this world to survive unless the tornays continued. After confirming once again that she had made the right decision, she rubbed her eyes and said wearily, 'Jax, please call a meeting for 07:00, including all commanders and tech personnel.'

'I will do so. Echo, Prowler II has left orbit.'

'Thank you. I am going to bed, call me if anything needs my attention.'

'I will do so. Good-eve, Echo.'

'And to you, my friend.'

TWENTY-FOUR:

The following morning, after wrestling most of the night with her decision, Echo arrived tired and out of sorts for the meeting in the conference room. The first person she saw as she entered was Relic, who was frowning and dare she say it looking concerned. With a nod of her head, she motioned to the person who had put that look on her face.

Echo's mouth fell open and her heart thumped hard when she saw Judge seated between Mayton and Ziv. Instinctively, she growled and slammed her tablet down on the table. Relic sighed in relief when she saw it was one of the new indestructible tablets everyone had been issued with.

Echo pulled her seat out and snapped, 'May I inquire why you are not aboard Prowler II, as I thought you would be?'

Judge was no fool. He could see Echo was angry. During his comm with Larson the previous night, Larson had explained tactics for disarming terrans before a problem could escalate. He gave her a rakish smile and inclined his head, 'You may.'

Drumming her fingers on the table, she snapped, 'This is me inquiring.'

Judge's grin grew as he leaned back in his chair and tried out one of the terran sayings he had heard from Marlo. 'Did you get up on the wrong side of the bed this morn?'

Temper blazed in Echo's eyes for a second, then her usual sense of humor reasserted itself and she slyly replied. 'Yes, and no. Unfortunately, I was alone, and that always makes me grumpy.'

Slamming upright, Judge snarled. 'Female, stop saying things like that. You will turn my hair white.'

'Is that so?'

'Indeed, my friends Larson and Marlo have told me of you

terrans and your conniving ways to make us crazy.'

'Conniving,' growled all the females.

Echo demanded, 'Stop talking to them. Their advice is bad.'

Judge shrugged as he had seen the females do. 'Not going to happen.'

'So wrong, I should never have put you in contact with them.'

Judge laughed then said, 'As if you could remain quiet.'

'Shut up.'

He shook his head, 'So rude. You need lessons in politeness.'

Echo eyeballed a smirking Relic as she whined, 'Stop listening to Relic.' When that only produced more smiles, she turned her attention to the other people waiting for her to address them. 'Thank you all for coming. After hours of combing through tedious amounts of information sent to me by my dedicated technical personnel.' Kido giggled as Haruto smiled at her description of the information they had given her, 'Anyway, I have formulated a plan to keep this world viable. But first, let's hear your reports.'

Avery delivered her report first. 'Medical treated all the fighters and they have gone with Prowler II. Commander Dinas is to continue any further treatment needed at home.'

'And the citizens?'

Avery sighed, 'Treatment is ongoing. It seems healers have not been welcomed here for several yentas.'

Charis muttered, 'Another way to drive the people from their world.'

Avery agreed, 'Yes, that is what we have been told over and over by the people of Otera Major.'

Echo nodded and asked, 'Anything else?'

'Only that they are going to need healers on a permanent basis. Are we doing anything about that?'

Echo acknowledged her concern, 'Yes, I have that covered.'

Avery breathed a sigh of relief. 'Good. So that was my report.'

Echo looked around at the others, 'Thanks, Avery. Anyone else?'

Ziv stood and smiled. 'As with Avery's patients, all mine were transferred to Prowler II under Kail Jarrod's care. He has advised me that more Mystics from all disciplines will arrive within days.'

Echo frowned. 'Tell me, Ziv, was it you or Kail Jarrod's recommendation for the extra Mystics?'

'It was mine, and he agreed with me.'

'What was your reasoning?'

'I believe these people will need the aid of Mystics to help rebuild this world, if that is your intention. If not, they will help the people cope with leaving.'

'I see. Well, I can add nothing to that. As with Avery, these were your patients.'

Ziv nodded, then sat again, his mind on the expression on Echo's face. Had he stepped on her toes as Lady Helen was fond of saying? He decided to speak to Relic later.

Next was Cleo, who stood and reported. 'We have lifted the lockdown and the chefs are supplying meals and providing food. The Prowler II added what they had with them and Amahka Kardan said more is on its way along with growing houses. We have had to quell one or two fights and a few rebellions. But in truth, it is just the fear of the unknown that is the driving force behind the spurts of protest. My people, along with Mayton's, are still patrolling the streets and helping to reassure anyone when it is needed but they are not troopers. So, I hope you have a plan for that because we cannot leave until we have some kind of structure in place that is not fear based.'

As she retook her seat, Echo said, 'I agree, Cleo, a presence will be needed here for some time. In fact, personnel are on their way who will fulfill all your requirements. Anything else?'

Relic stood and made her report. 'I have been notified the family we took on board has been treated and sent back down to the world.'

Surprised, Avery asked. 'She does not want to stay with us?'

Relic smiled as she recounted part of the conversation she had with the female. 'No, this is her home, and she just wanted justice and hope. She says now the Star Daughter has provided both, she is happy to remain on her world.'

Echo stood as Relic took her seat again. 'Good, we will need people like her. So, any other business?' When there was none, Echo outlined her plans. 'So this is my vision for the world of Otera Major. Now, as much as we may find tornays abhorrent—'

Ziv interrupted to ask, 'Excuse me, Echo, but do we really think that?'

Echo looked at Judge and said, 'Ahh, I thought so.'

Judge climbed slowly to his feet, 'As to that. I and many others do not feel that way. Before I was captured and held prisoner, I often competed in tornays.'

Echo blinked several times as she looked around at the faces staring at him. 'Can I ask why?'

Judge smiled and inclined his head. 'To test myself against other combatants. I enjoyed it.'

Relic grinned at Echo's expression and burst out laughing as Cleo said from where she sat. 'I also have fought in underground tornays.' At the surprised expressions turned her way, she clarified for the non-terrans. 'On Earth, of course, not since coming out here.'

Relic nudged her sister, 'Are you saying you never pitted yourself against anyone other than me when we lived on Earth?'

Uncomfortable with where this was going, Echo muttered. 'Well, no, I fought in underground bouts. But this is not about me.' She looked at Judge. 'It seems my assumption you would be against tornays was incorrect.'

Judge retook his seat as he told her, 'I understand how you came to that conclusion. I enjoyed my time as a fighter before the Emperor took me hostage. My experience since has not changed that. What I and my competitors disliked was the lack of rules and the hardship we experienced. We were not slaves or savgells to be traded and killed if we did not perform the way we were expected to.'

Charis asked, 'Can you explain why you were not killed?' At his raised eyebrow, she hurriedly said, 'I am thankful you were not, but you had lost most of your sight and hand.'

Echo asked, 'Yeah, how did that happen?'

Relic muttered, 'So rude!'

'Zip it, sister,' snarled Echo in return.

Judge looked at Charis and smiled. 'The Emperor and his brother soon discovered it was wiser to keep me around than have me executed.'

Still confused, Avery asked, 'Yeah, but why?'

Judge shrugged. 'I was the only one who could stop the fighters from killing themselves.'

Avery yelped. 'What does that mean?!'

'Healer Avery, many fighters would take their own lives rather than be tortured in the cage.'

'Oh my stars, that is so sad.'

'It is, and something I hope will be remedied.'

Echo whispered to Relic, 'It will be and quickly if I have anything to say about it.'

With a grimace, Relic replied, 'That's for sure.'

Echo cleared her throat and stated, 'I am appalled by what Judge has told us and vow to stop that and any other practices we deem wrong.'

Ziv asked, 'How?'

Echo raised her eyebrows. 'By taking over the running of Otera Major. The people of this world need the tornays, but what they don't need is the unethical practices that seem to be rampant in the sport. So I purpose we build on what the Emperor wanted to do except we incorporate the citizens of Otera Major to help.'

'Again I ask, how?'

Echo grinned. 'It's just as well I like you, Ziv.' After the laughter subsided, she continued, 'This will be done by establishing an Embassy here and granting permission for other worlds to do likewise. We will control the world and rule it by the principles of the Star Daughter's ethos. I also hope that in time it will become the place to watch competitive fights, sports and entertainment. Anything that is legal.'

Relic asked, 'Will the competitions be open to females?'

'I would hope the administrator we put in place agrees with female fighters.'

Cleo asked, 'Will you allow pleasure houses?'

Echo shrugged, 'That will be up to the person or persons overseeing the world, but I think if they were willing, then Otera Minor would be ideal for that. But again, it would be bound to the Star Daughter's ethos.'

Mayton said as he looked admiringly at Echo, 'You seem to have thought this out carefully.'

'I thank you. I know I have not covered everything, but this is the bare bones, so to speak of what the Star Daughter wants here and its sound if we put in place the infrastructure with administration.'

Relic agreed, 'It is a good plan, Echo, but who is going to oversee the restructuring and safeguard the citizens, as well as install ethics to the tornays? It is a big ask of anyone.'

'I know, Relic, I would be asking someone to take on a gigantic challenge which could take yentas to accomplish.'

Judge leaned back in his chair as he told the silent room, 'One I am fully prepared to do.'

Relic's shock was palpable as she leaned forward in her seat, her voice trembling with agitation. 'Judge, you want to remain here on this world after everything that has happened. No... No, I don't think you should. Let someone who was not imprisoned here do it.'

Judge looked from one sister to the other before telling her, 'Sweet Relic, I am the right person and for all the reasons you just named and many more. This is what I was created to do, bring justice to the enslaved, to right the wrongs in my Star Daughter's name.'

Relic pleaded with Echo, 'Stop him. This is not the reason we saved him. It seems cruel.'

Echo shook her head. 'I am not telling a grown male Warrior what he can and cannot do.' When Relic went to speak, she said, 'Sister, would you refuse a challenge of this magnitude? Did you ever?'

Relic slumped back in her chair as she said, 'No, no, I would not.'

Judge left his seat and walked to stand next to Relic. He cupped her cheek as he gently assured her, 'Pretty Relic, I swear it is what I want.'

He saw the tears she refused to let fall as she covered his hand with her own. 'Okay, if this is what you want. As long as you understand, I do not have to like it. Also, we are only a comm away if you need us.'

He grinned as he told her, 'I know that, Relic.' When he returned to his seat, he explained, 'I plan to implement all of Echo's recommendations. Her future for this world is sound and will be in time profitable not only for the citizens but for the competitors as well as for the Star Daughter.'

Echo cleared her throat before she asked. 'I have to ask you officially, are you, Judge Shaw, willing to take over the administration of the world known as Otera Major?'

'Yes, I am so willing.'

Grinning with pleasure, she asked, 'Okay, so what title do you wish to use?'

'I will use Governor Judge Shaw.'

Avery cheered, 'Oh my stars, that is an impressive title.'

Cleo told him, 'It suits you. Wear it well.'

Echo and Relic agreed with her. Ziv quietly said, 'Honor the office, my friend.'

Echo inclined her head and stated, 'Judge Shaw, you are now the new governor of Otera Major—'

Judge interrupted her to say, 'I am changing the name of the world to Kelara.'

'Kelara, why?'

He shrugged, 'It was suggested to me.'

Echo sighed loudly before asking, 'What do you think the people will say?'

Cleo said, 'I think they will be more than willing to have a fresh start. A new name does that. And with everything else you are thinking of doing, it can only get better for them.

Restored pride for their home world can help to heal old wounds. Especially for those who the people feel abandoned them when things were hard.'

Charis asked her, 'You expect people to return after all this time?'

Cleo nodded, 'Yes, most will. Home is home.'

Cleo's words gave everyone something to think about and soon after, the meeting broke up. Only Judge and the two Wallace sisters remained behind. Judge spoke first, 'I should have told you.'

Relic asked, 'That you were talking to Peyton?'

He nodded. 'About that and my decision.'

Echo spoke up, 'Nah, we've all been there and truthfully, I wanted you for the position, anyway so it all ends well.' She looked over at Relic and said, 'We will miss you, though.'

She agreed, 'Yes, we will.'

Judge rocked back in his chair. 'As to that, I am only staying here until I have met all the challenges we decide on for the world and any personal ones I have. When I am satisfied, I can do no more, I will hand over the world to my successor and come home.'

Relic quipped, 'Or join us.'

'Or join you.'

Echo asked, 'But until then you will come and visit?'

'There is no reason you cannot visit here. Then we can travel to Maikonia together.'

Echo grinned, 'Oh good idea, then you cannot get lost.'

His tone was a little frosty when he assured Echo, 'I am a Warrior, and I never get lost.'

'No need to be offended, it was just a thought.'

'Please stop thinking.'

'And you say I am rude.'

'You are,' Returned Relic as she led Judge from the room.

TWENTY-FIVE:

Two weeks after Judge had been appointed Governor of Kelara, Echo decided to visit the planet. She had not been on the world since he had taken over, hoping the transfer of power to Judge would go smoother if she was not there as a distraction. So far, it seemed to be working.

What inspired her to want to visit the planet was a report she had read just that morning on the port. Feeling bored, the idea of doing some research of her own into making the port more inviting seemed like a good idea. To that end, she needed to get her sister on board, so to speak. In other words, not throw a hissy fit because she was leaving the ship.

Echo poked her head around the door to Relic's office. 'Relic, I am going to the planet.'

Relic looked up from her comp. 'Why are you bothering me?'

'Because last time I did something without telling you, first, you had a hissy fit.'

Relic was sure she was developing a twitch in her right eye. She rubbed her temple and hissed between clenched teeth, 'You entered a cell with an Elite.'

Echo affected a bored tone as she muttered loud enough for her sister to hear, 'Whatever, just remember I told you.'

Sighing loudly, Relic asked, 'Who is going with you? Because I cannot go, I am working here.'

'I did not ask you to. I was just telling—'

Relic quickly interrupted her, 'Whatever!'

'Ha-ha, so funny.'

'Take Charis.'

'Are you sure?'

'Last nerve, Echo.'

With a grin, Echo waved goodbye and left her sister with her eyes glued to her screen. She found Charis in the star lounge. 'Greetings Charis, I am going planet-side. Relic said you can come with me.'

Charis looked up from the book she was reading on her tablet, 'Oh, lucky me.'

'So funny. How long do you need?'

'Ten mins.'

'Okay, meet you in the shuttle bay.'

'Who else is going?'

'Just you and me.'

'Okay.'

Knowing Charis would take the entire ten minutes to prepare for her visit. Echo strolled to the shuttle bay and read the roster on who was on duty today. She smiled when she read Hoya Tyrrell's name, otherwise known as Ty. He was one of her favorite pilots. She liked him the first time he had come to a poker game with an unlit cigar dangling from the corner of his mouth and a baseball cap turned backwards on his head. He wore his blond hair shoulder-length and had a blue eye ring. She appreciated his sense of humor and his blunt way of speaking.

She wandered over to the shuttle in bay three and stood admiring its lines. This was one of the new crafts designed by Kolin. It had seats for only twelve people and was intended as a transporter between ships and planets. 'Are you on board, Ty?'

His reply from within the ship was as she expected, 'Where else would I be?'

'How the hayda would I know, which is why I asked if you were on board?'

As he stepped onto the ramp, he grinned. 'Grouchy this morn?'

'No more than usual.'

Ty came down the ramp and stopped next to Echo, causing her to look up at the handsome male and silently sigh with pleasure. 'How is it you are not mated yet?'

'Why must you ask me this each time I see you?'

'Guess I am just baffled.'

'Do you need transport or have you come to bust my chops?'

Echo laughed, 'No, I am not here to bust your chops, which is a disgusting saying.'

Ty grinned as he told her, 'Although it says everything that needs saying.'

'True, and I am here to get a ride to the planet.'

He frowned as he asked, 'You are not going alone, are you?'

'Nope, Charis is with me when she gets here.'

Ty looked up when he heard the bay doors open. 'That would be her now.'

Echo turned to see Charis fully kitted up bristling with weapons walking sedately to where they stood. 'Yep.'

'I will get clearance.' With that, Ty walked back into the shuttle, leaving Echo to greet Charis. 'All right then, Captain?'

'Ahh, yeah, I am fairly sure I covered everything.'

Eyeing her weapons, Echo said, 'You know. Cleo and Matt have secured the planet.'

Charis quoted a saying Relic often used, 'One cannot be too casual about the threat to the Negotiator.'

'Dearle stars, that sounds as if it is straight from the Relic handbook on guarding.'

Charis grinned as they both made their way into the shuttle before saying, 'It is.'

Echo shook her head. 'Save me now.'

Ty grinned and ordered, 'Get seated. We have permission to leave. Greetings, Charis.'

'Greetings, Ty.'

Unlike the other shuttles, that had seats arranged in rows like an airplane, the seats in this shuttle were positioned along the walls, leaving a large center aisle clear. This design, made it easier to walk around. As Echo took her seat, she asked Ty, 'How long until we are planet-side?'

Charis almost fell from her seat as she exclaimed, 'How do you not know that!?'

Echo shrugged as the harness moved into place over her. 'I was busy all the other times I went down. And Ty flies faster than the other pilots.'

'Oh.'

Fifteen minutes later, Ty piloted the shuttle into the docking bay Judge had assigned to the Negotiator. Several other shuttles were already docked in their own bays. 'You were right,' grinned Charis, 'that was the fastest time I have ever flown here.'

Echo grinned in return. 'Told you, the fastest pilot ever.'

As Ty ran his checks, he frowned while he scanned the empty port beyond the window of the shuttle. When the door didn't open, Charis asked him, 'Problem?' Causing Echo to look out at the empty port.

'No, it is just an unnatural feeling seeing an empty port.'

Charis grinned, 'Yeah, I get that spooky and all.'

'Spooky, what is this word?'

Echo explained, 'It means the same as sinister.'

'I said unnatural.'

'Whatever, flyboy.'

Ty's top lip quirked up in a smile. Then, with another scan of the port, told her, 'I will await you here.'

Echo was aghast, 'But you could get bored.'

He pulled a tablet from a drawer and enthusiastically told her, 'I am reading a book on the wild-wild-west. It is most exciting.'

'Well, if you are happy.'

Ty released the door and ramp but kept his eyes on the port. He could not name what was disturbing him, but it felt as though the very air was holding its breath, which heightened his sense of dread. As Echo and Charis began their trek down the ramp, he wanted to call them back. He couldn't shake the feeling that something was not right. His hands itched for a weapon as he scanned the port once more. He knew he could not sit and wait for their return. So he thumbed the secure pad on the wall behind his seat, removing the blaster from the hidden compartment. With that in hand, he crept from the shuttle.

Echo and Charis stepped down off the ramp and walked to the doors leading into the port. Looking around, Echo asked her, 'Do you have your tablet?'

Charis grinned, 'I do. Are we taking notes?'

With a laugh, Echo said, 'You are. I am just talking.'

As she removed her tablet from her inside jacket pocket, Charis asked, 'What are you going to talk about?'

'I want to see what I can do to make this port more user friendly.'

Looking around at the windowless dirt- brown walls and dull black floors, Charis muttered, 'Is it even possible?'

Echo shrugged as she pressed the button to open the doors and looked back over her shoulder at Charis. 'It is if we do away with the bars between the aisles and add some windows.'

Charis nodded. 'Change the color of the décor to add personality.'

'Exactly, the port needs to say welcome, not go away and never come back—'

'And that is exactly what you should do,' said a harsh male voice as several arrows thumped into Echo, pushing her back into Charis and toppling them both to the floor. Charis roared as she tried to disentangle herself from Echo's dead weight. **'Echo!?'**

Suddenly, there were pulsating sounds as bolts of energy flew from the blaster Ty held. He rushed to the door lock, ducking several bolts as they flew through the opening, and slapped a hand over the pad. Once the doors closed, he shot out the entry panel, rending the mechanism useless. He knew it would not take the males long to force the doors open, but by then he hoped to be long gone.

Turning back to the two females, his heart almost stopped in his chest when he saw the bolts in Echo's body. His voice was harsher than normal when he ordered, 'Move Charis.'

Her muffled reply was easily heard in the silence of the docking bays, 'I am trying.'

He laid his weapon down and gently lifted Echo's lax body off Charis, who quickly jumped to her feet. He checked her over, then told her, 'You are bleeding.'

'It's not my blood. How is she?'

'Still breathing. We have to go. It will not take them long to break through the door. Grab my weapon.'

Charis bent down and swiped the blaster off the floor and then ran to catch up with Ty, who was striding up the ramp. He lay Echo on the floor and hurried to retract the ramp and close the door as he started the shuttle's engine.

Breathlessly, Charis stood looking down at the arrows or bolts sticking from Echo. She counted fifteen before she realized the shuttle was moving. She looked at Ty and asked, 'What should I do?'

'Nothing. Comm the healers. They will know what you should or should not do. Tell them we are seven mins out.'

Shocked at the time he gave her, she squeaked, 'Seven mins!?'

His smile was grim as he nodded, 'Seven. Comm them now!'

Charis sat on the floor next to Echo and placed her fingers on her throat. Her pulse was weak and her breathing shallow. She tapped her link and nothing happened, she tapped it again and still nothing happened. 'Tuap.' She called out to Ty, 'My link is not working, is yours?'

He didn't reply, only ran his index finger down a small panel on the dash in front of him. 'Emergency override 092181, Pilot Hoya Tyrrell.'

Instantly Jax asked. 'Pilot Hoya, state your emergency.'

'We were ambushed when we made port. The Negotiator is severely wounded. We need medics on arrival. Tell the Commander I am coming in hot.'

'Understood. Estimated time of arrival?'

'Six mins.'

'Understood, link will remain open.'

Ty heaved a deep sigh as he replied, 'Thanks Jax.'

'Were you or Captain Charis wounded?'

'No.'

'Understood.'

TWENTY-SIX:

Relic scowled as Jax interrupted her, 'Commander.'

'Yes, Jax.'

'Negotiator Echo was ambushed at the port. She has been severely wounded. Her shuttle will arrive in five mins and thirty-seven seconds.'

Relic's heart thumped loudly and blood rushed to her head as she fearfully asked, 'Is she alive?'

'Yes.'

'And the pilot and Charis?'

'Unhurt.'

'Have you notified Avery?'

'I have, as well as Governor Shaw. Commander Gibson is securing the port.'

'Better late than never, I suppose,' muttered Relic.

Jax continued as though she had not spoken. 'Captain Mayton and his scouts are hunting as we speak.'

'Any clues who did this?'

'Pilot Ty did not say. I am awaiting more details from Commander Gibson or Governor Shaw.'

'How the Hayda did this happen?'

'I am unable to respond.'

'Rhetorical question. I will find out, I am sure. For now, Jax, please notify me when you know anything more.' Her voice hardened as she requested, 'Jax, have Commander Gibson report to me when she can, in person.'

He warned, 'It may take some time.'

'I understand, as soon as it is feasible.'

'Yes, Commander.'

'I will be in medical.'

'Understood.'

Jax watched her leave her office and then made a comm to Maikonia, 'Kardan.'

Kardan was seated behind his desk reading reports on the information gathered from the prisoners retrieved from Kelara. 'Yes, Jax, has something occurred?'

'There has been an incident on Kelara.'

'Report, please.'

As he had done earlier, Jax relayed what he knew of the ambush and the updated progress report on Echo. When he had finished, Kardan ran his hand through his hair and cursed. 'Dayam it to hayda. How the furin hayda did this happen? The planet was supposed to be secure!'

'Unfortunately, it appears to be an oversight.'

'Or overconfidence. Who is the Commander on the ground?'

'Commander Gibson.'

'Furin hayda. Comm command.'

'Will you tell Peyton?'

'Yes, notify me directly if there are any changes and keep me updated on Echo's progress.'

'Yes, Kardan.'

'Dayam it, Jax.' He sighed and then asked, 'How bad is she?'

'I believe her wounds are life threatening. They will not know until they remove the bolts.'

'Bolts?'

'Yes, it appears she was shot with crossbolts. Commander Gibson just reported they have captured three Raiders and killed ten more.'

'Raiders do not use bolts.'

'No, Captain Mayton reported a Raider has confessed they used Assaens. He did not know from what guild the Assaens were from.'

Kardan sighed, 'Assaen's hiring out to Raiders. Once I would have said this was most unlikely.'

Jax quietly agreed, 'As I would have.'

'Please ask Harm and Klune to meet us in conference room two.'

'Yes, Kardan.' After a minute, when neither of them said anything further, Jax said, 'Do not forget, she is a descendant of warriors.'

'I was just thinking that and it would be a great shame if we were to lose her.'

'Perhaps it would be a good idea not to say that to Peyton. Just tell her she is of warrior blood.'

'Yes, yes, good idea.'

'Kardan, you are not moving.'

'I know, I am fortifying myself.'

'I believe whiskay is needed for that.'

'True. Keep me posted, my friend.'

'I will.'

TWENTY-SEVEN:

Kardan made his way to Peyton's office. He braced himself and entered without his usual knock. Penny sat behind her desk, one look at his face, and she asked, 'Who do you need?'

'Jax is organizing them. We are assembling in conference room two.'

As she stood, she said, 'I will go there now.'

'Thank you.'

With a nod, she watched him enter Peyton's office. Peyton turned from the dispenser and, as with Penny, she took one look at his face and asked, 'Who?'

'You know once I could walk into a room and no one knew what I was thinking or feeling.'

'They were not terran. You are stalling, my heart.'

'Echo was ambushed at the port.'

'Anyone else hurt?'

'No.'

Peyton felt every muscle in her body tighten as she asked him, 'How bad is she?'

'Life threatening, they hit her with bolts.'

'Crossbolts, what the hayda?'

Kardan nodded. 'An unusual weapon for Raiders.'

'You are sure it was Raiders?'

'So Jax reported.'

Peyton asked, 'Are you thinking Assaen's working with Raiders?'

'As unlikely as that seems, yes.'

'I see. Relic?'

'I do not know.'

Peyton stared into Kardan's sympathetic eyes as she asked, 'Jax, how is Relic?'

'Incandescent with rage and guilt.'

'Dayam, that's not good. Progress on Echo, please?'

'She is in surgery.'

'Thank you, keep us informed.'

'I will.'

She asked Kardan, 'So, thoughts?'

'What I want to do is take a Warbird to the planet and—' He grimaced, 'you know the rest. Instead, I have called a conference with command and invited Klune and Harm to participate.'

'Okay.' She walked into his waiting arms and looked up into his beautiful face and told him, 'She will be okay. She comes from warrior blood.'

He smiled as he kissed her softly and whispered, 'I was going to use that to comfort you.'

She returned the kiss, then shrugged, although he could see the concern haunting her eyes. 'I want to go to her.'

Kardan placed his cheek on top of her head as he held her. 'But we cannot. We trusted them enough to go to the planet without us. Now we have to trust them to fix this.'

Peyton closed her eyes and sighed. 'I know. They will have to own the fallout from whatever went wrong, but it will not be easy. However, it unfolds.'

Kardan agreed, 'As it should not be. Someone failed and they have to learn how and why they did so.'

She pulled from his arms as she asked, 'In your opinion, what went wrong?'

'Overconfidence and perhaps failure on my part in not sending more seasoned Warriors with them.'

'But then, how do they become seasoned if they always have someone to rely on?'

He sighed and agreed, 'That is true.'

'No, this is on them. The fault lies with the Commanders and now as Commanders they have to find out where they screwed up.'

'Harsh lessons.'

Peyton shrugged, 'Yes, and Echo paid for their

mismanagement.'

Kardan agreed and said, 'There may have to be demotions.'

Peyton grimaced at the idea. 'Perhaps.'

Kardan asked with a half-smile, 'You do not like the thought of that.'

'No, they worked so hard to achieve their ranks. Stripping them of it is demoralizing, and not just for them but for everyone who cheered them on and had faith in them. No, let's not go down that road. I think once the dust settles, there will be enough regrets to go around and they will be stronger for it.'

'I hope you are right.'

Peyton murmured a heartfelt. 'Me too!' She placed her hand in his, and they walked to the door. Before opening it, she said, 'I hate this.'

Kardan squeezed her hand lightly as he agreed. 'I have to say I do not relish this either. Let us go talk to our people and find out what and who we are up against.'

'Yes, because as sure as the suns will rise tomorrow, there is something or someone behind this.'

TWENTY-EIGHT:

Relic paced the hallway outside medical as Jax reported on the progress made on the planet. Rage burned a hole in her stomach and no matter how hard she rubbed it, she could not lessen the feeling of guilt that wanted to swallow her.

'Commander, do you want coffee?'

'What? Oh Charis, I am sorry. What did you ask?'

'Do you want coffee?'

'No, no, nothing thanks.' She turned and paced to the end of the hall and stared sightlessly out the window. She turned when the lift doors opened and saw Judge exit, his expression concerned. Relic harshly demanded, 'What are you doing here?'

'I am where I am needed to be.'

'The Raiders?'

'Are all in custody or dead. Intercessor's Commander is on alert.'

'Why?'

'The Raiders told us there are ships expected within days.'

'Do you believe them?'

'No, but we will remain on alert.'

'Okay.'

'Commander Gibson has the planet on lockdown once more and is continuing her door-to-door search.'

'Why, if they have captured all the Raiders?'

Judge told her, 'The weapon used is an Assaen's tool.'

'You are saying Assaens are working with the Raiders?'

'Until we know something different, yes.'

Relic tipped her head to the side and concluded. 'From that answer, I would be right in saying none have been captured so far.'

'Correct.'

'So they could do it again.'

'Commander Gibson is aware of this.'

By now, Judge stood before her. She looked up into his eyes and whispered, 'I cannot lose her. I made it through my mother's death because of Echo. I fear no one will be safe from me if she dies. My revenge will have no bounds.'

'I understand, Relic, but remember you are not alone. You have me and our homeworld to stand with you. And your rage, I fear, will be nothing to our Star Daughter's and Amahkas. So let us hope she survives, for I fear there will be worlds that will not.'

She flung herself into his arms, 'Oh, Judge.'

'Hush now,' he soothed as he held her, gaining as much comfort from her as she did from him.

An hour later, Avery walked from surgery and smiled when she saw Relic and Judge holding hands. Relic quickly stood, 'How is she?'

'Well—'

Relic held her hand up to stop the healer talking. 'Can you wait until Ty and Charis get here?' Just then, the door opened to admit the couple. 'Oh good, you are here. Avery was just going to tell us how she is.'

Avery nodded to the couple, then said, 'She is well, and is in the regen now where she will remain for an hour. You may sit with her.'

'We would like that. Thank you, Avery.'

She waved her thanks away as she told them, 'She is a fighter. It must be all that Wallace blood you all go on about.'

Relic grinned with relief as she rejoined, 'So funny.'

Charis asked, 'How many bolts did you pull from her?'

'Twenty-one.'

Ty whistled as Judge grunted and Charis blurted, 'Holy shit!'

Shocked and grateful, Relic muttered, 'I second that.'

After a moment in which they all contemplated Echo's luck and strength, Judge asked Jax, 'Jax, let everyone know Echo is well and recovering.'

'Yes, Governor.' Jax was relieved by the news that his new

friend was recovering. He was amused by her remarkable ability to inject humor into any given situation, and he greatly admired how she projected an outward image that contradicted her inner struggles. He pondered whether she realized just how much Peyton depended on her to accomplish the tasks set forth by the Star Child.

He found Peyton and Kardan still in the conference room. 'Madam Peyton, I have an update on Negotiator Echo.'

'Thank you, Jax, what is it?'

'She has successfully survived surgery and is now in the regen where she will remain for the next two hours.'

Peyton was as relieved as everyone else in the room. Kardan squeezed her hand as she cleared her throat before saying, 'Please give our thanks to Healer Avery and reassure Relic we are here if she needs us.'

'I will convey both messages.'

Harm asked Jax, 'Do they know how many bolts they fired?'

'Healer Avery reported she removed twenty-one bolts. How many were actually fired is still undetermined.'

Klune's shocked exclamation caught everyone's attention, 'Impossible!'

Netta asked, 'Is there a problem?'

Harm shook his head, 'No, we are stunned. Actually, more than stunned, we have never heard of anyone surviving so many bolts.'

Klune agreed, 'We have known some to survive five bolts, but twenty-one, never. It is a miracle.'

Peyton smiled as she said. 'Or the power of determination.'

Marlo asked, 'What does that mean?'

Netta explained, 'It means Echo Wallace has much to accomplish for us and herself. She would not so easily surrender to an Assaen's bolt.'

Harm asked Jax, 'Please ensure the bolts are preserved. We will need to examine them.'

'I have done so. Captain Mayton took charge of the evidence.'

'I thought he would.'

Bendrix asked Harm, 'What do you expect to learn from the bolts?'

'There are only two worlds who use bolts as their tool of death. When I have inspected the bolts, I will know what world is taking commissions from the Raiders.'

Peyton nodded as she said, 'Then I will talk to them and ask them why they thought taking a commission to kill my Negotiator was a wise choice.'

Klune asked, 'And if you do not receive a satisfactory answer.'

Kardan stated, 'Then we will visit their world and ask their leaders. I am sure they will wish to explain it to me.'

'Hold a min,' said Netta. 'Why can you not just ask the Assaens themselves when Cleo captures them?'

'Two reasons,' explained Harm, 'they will have left the world or be dead by now.'

'Dead?'

'Yes, Netta, dead. They will not wish to be captured and definitely not by us.'

Klune agreed. 'They only have two options: run or die.'

'Oh.' Netta looked at Peyton, who shrugged.

Kardan clarified, 'It is a harsh Universe.'

Netta grinned as she told them, 'Oh, I am not complaining, just taken aback at how feared our Assaens are. Who knew?'

Harm snarled, 'So funny.'

TWENTY-NINE:

Relic sat beside the regen tube and watched the holes in her sister's skin close and her color return to normal. 'This was close.'

Judge agreed, 'Too close.'

'Someone was behind this,' murmured Mayton as he stepped into the room.

Relic agreed. 'Any ideas?'

'No, but I know command thinks the same and are working on who it could be.'

Relic frowned as she posed a question. 'So Mayton, let me ask you, is it typical to use that many bolts?'

'It was excessive.'

Relic looked away from her sister and at the male leaning against the wall. 'What do you mean?'

'Harm told me two is standard. He has heard of someone surviving five, twenty-one is excessive.'

Judge rubbed his cheek as he murmured, 'So someone targeted her, wanting to make sure she died.'

Mayton nodded in agreement. 'That is the feeling from Harm and Lord Klune.'

Anger lit Relic's eyes. 'That will be their undoing. We Wallace's do not forget or forgive. These people have no idea who they have unleashed.'

'Easy there, Relic.'

She turned burning eyes on Judge. 'Easy… there is no easy. There is only retribution.'

Silence descended on the room and a few minutes later, Judge and Mayton excused themselves leaving Relic with her guilt and anger as she sat vigil by her sister.

As they left the medical unit, Judge sighed. 'Furin hayda, this will not end well for the ones responsible for this.'

Mayton grinned, 'No, although I think I am going to request to accompany the sisters as they hunt for the ones responsible.'

Judge also grinned at Mayton's enthusiastic tone. 'I believe I will leave that to you, but I will ask a favor of you.'

'Which I will grant if I can.'

Judge stopped walking and turned to the younger male. 'Keep me informed. You may need my counsel.'

'Goes without saying. If I am assigned to Echo, I will report what we discover.'

'Thank you.'

An hour later, Echo turned her head on the pillow as the lid of the regen tube hissed open. 'Hey, sis.'

Relic smiled and if there were a few unshed tears glistening her eyes, neither sister mentioned them. 'Hey, yourself.'

'So, I have a question.'

'What?'

'How come there are not a lot of brothers in the Warriors? I know the Roeahs are brothers and Kerol and Lukkas, but that is about it. Why is that do you think?'

Judge, on hearing the question as he entered the room with Avery, asked Relic, 'Is she addled?'

Echo gave him a narrowed-eyed stare as she asked him, 'What the hayda does that mean, addled?'

Judge asked her in return, 'Are you confused or did a bolt cause you to become insane?'

Huffily Echo grumbled, 'Whatever! If you do not know the answer, just say so. No need to get nasty.'

'Dear stars, you are insane. One of those bolts hit your head.'

'No, they did not and I am not insane. It is a legitimate question. One I have been thinking about for a while.'

'Enough, please,' ordered Relic as Avery gasped for breath. 'Stop laughing, Avery.'

'Sorry... sorry.' She went to help Echo from the regen. 'You can get up now. But I warn you, Echo you have to take it easy for the next few days. And by easy, I mean do absolutely nothing but eat, sleep, walk slowly and sit often for the next four days.'

'Whatever you say.'

Avery placed a hard hand on her shoulder as she made to get off the bed. 'Echo, I mean it, ignore my warning and I will sedate you into compliance.'

Echo looked at her friend and saw the concern clouding her eyes and squeezed her hand. 'I will, I promise.' She sneered at Judge. 'Contrary to popular opinion, I am not insane. I know I need time to finish healing.'

'All right.'

'Thanks Avery, for everything. I have a feeling I would not have survived if it wasn't for you and your team. So thank them for me, please.'

'I will, but the most thanks should go to and Ty and Charis, they got you here so I and my team could keep you alive.'

Echo smiled as she assured her, 'I will be thanking them too. But for now, I want a shower and, funnily enough, some rest.'

Avery smiled as she explained, 'It is normal, now go to your cabin.'

Echo moved closer to Avery and told her, 'You see how close death is to us?' She looked her friend in the eyes and said, 'Death does not give us the luxury of time so we must grab all the love we can while we live. So, I say stop worrying and go talk to Mayton.'

Avery bit her lip and then nodded, 'You are right. It is time to stop worrying over stupid things.'

Echo looked over at Relic who had been unashamedly listening and smirked, 'Then you can be like Relic.'

'Shut up, Echo!'

THIRTY:

Later that night, Avery stood outside Mayton's cabin door and clenched her hands until her knuckles turned white. She whispered, 'I am such a coward. Why is this so hard?'

'Perhaps you are trying too hard,' said a voice from behind her.

Turning slowly, she encountered Peyton, who smiled gently. Avery whispered, 'It should be simple. I love him. My heart beats for him. I dream of him every night, look for signs of him every min of every day, and yet when it comes time to declare my love for him, I freeze.'

Peyton smiled and the blue of her eyes blazed. 'Avery, sweet Avery, she who cares for the ailing and wounded, release the fears you carry. Remember, the Star Child sent you the perfect male, a male who will worship and love you forever. Open the door to your future, to a future you deserve.'

Avery nodded and took a breath and turned to the door, then remembered she had not thanked Peyton, but when she looked back, the passageway was empty. 'Thank you, Peyton. Here goes nothing.'

Peyton's voice whispered across her mind. *No, sweet Avery, here comes everything.*

'Let's hope so.' With a determined tilt to her chin, she opened the door and stared at a half-naked Mayton. Now, what she wanted to say was greetings Mayton. What she said instead was. 'Mayton Norr. I am your future.'

Mayton dropped the shirt he was holding and a slow, sexy smile blessed his handsome face. 'Yes, you are. Close the door, my heart.'

Avery let go a nervous giggle and stepped inside the cabin, closing the door silently behind her.

Delighted at the outcome, Peyton returned to her body and when she opened her eyes, Netta asked, 'Were you successful?'

'Yes, Avery has her mate and Mayton has his heart.'

Netta sighed with pleasure. She liked both Mayton and Avery and had hoped for a match between the two. She said now, 'They deserve to be happy.'

Peyton rubbed her hands with glee as she told Netta, 'I cannot wait to tell Brenda she has another ceremony to arrange.'

Netta inspected her nails as she said, 'You may want to hold off on that.'

Peyton frowned as she asked suspiciously, 'Why?'

Netta looked up from her nails, her grin turning into a full-blown smile as she explained, 'Matt and Relic should declare their undying love for each other as soon as she returns home.'

Shocked, Peyton opened and closed her mouth several times before uttering one word.

'What?'

'You heard. Matt and Relic.'

'But how did this happen?'

'Star Child, love, mates. You know the usual reasons.'

Peyton dropped her head into her palms. 'Yeah, yeah. Only, I'm not sure Matt is ready for a mate. He just bonded with Shade.'

'So, you think he should wait? That they both should wait?'

Peyton nodded emphatically, scrambling for a reason that would make sense to not only Netta but herself. 'Yes, that is probably for the best. I mean, Relic has just gone on her first mission.' She pleaded with Netta, 'You see, the implications here?'

Netta stood as she told her sister, 'You know all of that is tuap. You just don't like the idea of Matt finding a mate and especially not one who leaves home as much as Relic is going to.'

Peyton growled when she heard Netta put her feelings into words. 'Since when did you start analyzing me?'

'Since I became your sister. You know I am right.'

'No, you are not, it's just—'

'You love Matt and want him to stay home where you can

make sure he stays safe. And you'd miss him.'

Peyton's face softened, 'Yeah, I would.' Then she snarled, 'But that is not the reason.'

Netta walked to the door. 'Sure it is. You have to let him go and you know Relic is the only person who will cope with both Matt's and Shade's abilities without freaking out.' She smirked as she said, 'Then again, I would love to see you tell Matt and Relic they are unsuited for each other at this time. Then watch you deal with both Wallace sisters and a pissed off falear and his bondmate.'

'Umm, no, I don't think anyone is ready for that.' Peyton sighed heavily, 'They do make a good couple and Matt really does deserve someone like Relic. She will defend him to the death.'

Netta agreed, 'As he will her.' She looked at Peyton and noticed the tiny smile. 'You almost sound relieved you have a good reason to do nothing. You wouldn't be scared of the sisters, would you?'

'Why would I be?'

'Oh, no reason, it's just we have both seen examples of their fighting skills.'

Peyton shrugged nonchalantly, 'So?'

'It was just a thought.'

Peyton ordered Netta, 'Well, Knife girl, you just keep your dayam thoughts to yourself.'

'You are scared?'

Peyton's response was immediate. 'Terrified.'

They both grinned as Netta said, 'Come on, and let me buy you a coffee. It will make all your cares float away.'

Peyton pouted, 'You say that, but it never happens.'

Netta slung her arm around Peyton's shoulders and whispered, 'Which is why we keep trying.'

'Oh, good point.'

THIRTY- ONE:

Two days after the attack on Echo, Commander Cleo Gibson strode purposefully into Relic's office and snarled, 'You ordered me here?' But before Relic could speak, she stated, 'Which you had no right to do. I am not under your command as much as you would like that to be so.'

Relic smirked as she stood, 'And yet you are here.'

Not the least bit intimidated, Cleo warned. 'Ease up, Relic.' Anger and guilt sat heavily on her shoulders as she asked, 'Why am I here?'

Relic raised her eyebrows as she said, 'I am waiting for you to tell me how you could let Echo's attack happen?'

'How I let it happen? I think that is a bit rich coming from you.'

Anger made her voice harsh as Relic drilled into Cleo's guilt. 'It was your furin mission to secure the planet and hunt out any Raiders that could, or as we now know were, hiding. To make it safe. You failed in your task.'

Cleo slammed her hands on the desk as Relic's shot hit home, and it hurt. She liked Echo, and she knew what Relic said was true. She had failed, she'd become too complacent, and Echo had paid for that. Relic's eyes narrowed in renewed anger as Cleo condemned her in return. 'I am not the only one at fault here, Commander. You had one task which was to oversee the safety of the Star Daughter's Negotiator and you failed. So, to my way of thinking, there is enough blame to go around.'

'Fuck you, Cleo.'

'And you too, Relic.'

'I think—'

'Shut up, Echo!' They both yelled as they looked at her standing in the doorway, with Glenn and Charis behind her.

Relic told her, 'This has nothing to do with you.'

'Whatever, I just came to tell you they have ordered us home. I thought you would like to know so you can start doing your leaving stuff.'

Cleo asked before Relic could, 'Why?'

Echo explained, 'The other Battlecruisers have arrived, and we have been relieved, but hey you two can keep on arguing, it was entertaining.'

'Shut up, Echo,' they both snapped again.

Relic snarled at Cleo, 'This will keep.'

'Anytime, little girl,' Cleo snarled right back and then brushed past Echo with a wink that almost had her laughing.

Looking over at Relic, she grinned and smirked. 'Nice one, Relic, making friends wherever we go.'

'Shut up, Echo.'

THIRTY-TWO:

It took a further ten days before the Intercessor could leave orbit for Maikonia. Echo stood in the star lounge watching the world of Kelara grow smaller as the Battlecruiser powered through space toward home.

Relic watched her for a moment before saying, 'You are going to miss him.'

Without turning, she asked, 'Aren't you?'

'Yes, but I am happy to be going home.'

Echo sighed as she rubbed her chest. 'Yeah, me too, but I have a small ache.'

Relic slung her arm around her sister. 'I know, hon, but Judge is happy. Just look at the changes he's made already. He got the people to agree to change their world's name without bloodshed.'

'True.'

'Then there are the education centers and medical centers that are already up and running.'

'Again, true.'

'He has sent out notifications to all the worlds, letting them know of the leadership change and that the tornays will continue, albeit in a different format.'

'You are right.'

'The male knows how to organize.'

Echo agreed, 'I know, and with the personnel Command sent, he's going to have that world up and running in no time.'

'Yep, give him another yenta and we won't recognize the place.'

Echo asked for reassurance, which wasn't long in coming, 'It's good, right? My plan, it will make a difference, and keep people alive?'

Relic hugged her. 'Yes. You saw what was possible and made it happen. Don't doubt yourself now. You were created for this role you've taken on. I am proud of you.' She looked at Echo and quietly stated. 'Mom would be proud of you.'

Echo whispered huskily. 'Thanks.'

As Relic turned her from the window, she asked. 'So do you think you'd join a tornay someday?'

Echo initial reaction was to scoff at the idea but as she thought about it, she liked the idea. 'You know. I just might. It would be a challenge.'

Relic grinned as she murmured. 'I know. Come on, let's see what delights await us in the diner.'

'I am seriously not eating her food again.'

Relic shrugged. 'Chef Helen assigned Enid to us.'

'Which I will correct when we return. I am tired of the complaints.'

'Well, don't worry about it. I heard Enid is in bed with a migraine or something so Sue is cooking.'

Relieved, Echo muttered a prayer, 'Thank the stars for small mercies.'

'It's not so bad, sis, we only have four days until we return to Maikonia and our life.'

Echo muttered, 'I thought this was our life now.'

'And what a glorious one it is!' Relic returned. Watching the sadness fade from Echo's eyes she grinned and said, 'So, did I tell you about Mayton and Avery?'

Echo laughed before asking, 'Did she finally propose?'

Relic chuckled. 'Not only that, but she is wearing tatts.'

'Finally. So, sis, has she inspired you to—'

'Shut up!'

'I'm just saying.'

Relic dropped her arm from Echo's shoulder and stomped from the star lounge. 'I'm not having this conversation with you.'

Echo quickly followed. 'But—'

'No, and shut up!'

THIRTY-THREE:

Matt and Shade entered the scouts lounge, only to see Sedeen and Cobalt sitting outside on the patio. 'Greetings, Sedeen, Cobalt.'

Sedeen looked up from his tablet. 'Greetings, Matt, Shade,' Cobalt greeted them both as well.

Matt asked, 'Is there coffee?'

Sedeen motioned to the urn sitting on the table. 'Yes, grab a cup.' He watched his friend as he helped himself to coffee. 'So, they return tomorrow?'

With one hand on Shade's back and the other wrapped around his mug of coffee, Matt affirmed Sedeen was correct. 'Yes.'

'What are you going to do?'

Smiling as he scratched behind Shade's ear, he shrugged, 'What I have to.'

Sedeen looked across the table and smirked. 'I did tell you love would find a way.'

Matt eyed his smug friend. 'I do not remember you saying that.'

'Perhaps I did not use those exact words, but I was right.'

He sipped from his cup as Matt shook his head and retorted, 'No, I remember you telling me I was loveable and desired by all females.'

Sedeen snorted the mouthful of coffee and made choking noises. When he got himself under control once more, he told him. 'Your memory is faulty, my friend. I said nothing remotely like that.' They both grinned and Sedeen asked, 'Have you decided which Wallace sister it is yet?'

'How do you know it is one of the sisters?'

'Matt, why do you ask these questions? Just accept I know

everything.'

Cobalt asked. *Why then, do you keep losing bets?*

'Whose side are you on?'

Obviously not the winning one.

Exasperated, Sedeen snarled, 'Why do I keep you around?'

Smugly, Cobalt replied. *You love me.*

'That can change.'

Cobalt stood and stretched, then gave Shade a nod. *We are going to the pool.* Together, the Prowlers left, leaving the two males to themselves. When the door closed behind them, Sedeen asked Matt, 'Seriously, how are you?'

'I am well. I have been in contact with Echo, and she has given me some insight into my mate.'

'I am pleased. Is there anything I can help you with?'

'No, I have it under control.'

'Are you sure?'

'Yes, I am sure. Why are you concerned? Have you heard something?'

'Me, hear something, like what?'

Matt shrugged. 'I do not know.'

Barely suppressing his glee, Sedeen said thoughtfully, 'Now that you mention it, there is a rumor going around about a male fitting your description shaking his body at all times of the day and night.'

Matt exclaimed, 'It is dancing. I am dancing, not shaking my body.'

Sedeen's glee spilled over as he chortled. 'Dancing... Is that what you call it?'

Matt snarled, 'Hate you so much.'

THIRTY- FOUR:

The following day the Intercessor arrived just after second sunrise. As was custom, Echo and Relic were taken from the ship to Maikonia in their own shuttle. Once strapped in, Relic asked Echo, 'Who do you report to?'

'No one, it is one of the perks of being the Negotiator. I just had to send in my account of my adventures since we left home and that was that.'

'Echo that is a report.'

'So says you.'

'No, so says everyone.'

'Whatever.'

'You will still have to see Kardan about the attack.'

Echo shrugged, unconcerned. 'I know, but not immediately. I have to get my house in order first.'

'What does that mean?'

'It means resettle into Maikonian life, then interview people for permanent positions with the Intercessor.'

'Are you going to ask Cleo to return?'

'Should I?'

Relic slowly nodded, 'Yes, she is exceptionally intelligent and has more street sense than any other person except for us that I know.'

Frowning, Echo asked, 'But you are not talking to her. You and she have avoided each other for days now.'

'I know. We will work it out now we are home.'

'Okay, just, you know, make sure there is no breaking anybody while you are sorting it out. I need you both.'

'Thanks for your vote of confidence.'

'Hey, I was being confident, for you.'

'Whatever!'

THIRTY-FIVE:

Later that afternoon, after Echo had caught up on all her chores and made an appointment at the local beauty salon, she made her way to her office only to be halted before reaching it by Netta. 'Greetings.'

'And to you, Netta.'

Netta looked her over and nodded. 'You look well.'

Echo agreed, 'I am, thank you.'

'Have you been to medical for your after-mission health check?'

Echo scratched her cheek as she hesitantly asked, 'Ahh… no, was I meant to?'

Frowning, Netta just stopped herself from growling. 'Yes, all personnel receive them on returning to Maikonia.'

'Oh, okay, I'll go there now.' She turned and began her trek from the Hex. She looked to the side and found Netta pacing with her. Amused, she asked, 'So what can I do for you, Netta?'

'Bendrix is worried.'

'And this concerns me how?'

Netta's frown became darker as she explained. 'He is worried about you.'

'And again I ask, this concerns me how?'

'It is bad enough Peyton and the others worry, but when my Bendrix does, it has to stop.'

Echo halted and looked at the female. 'Netta, just say it. You are driving me insane and I have been accused of that already. I found it disturbing.'

Netta muttered. 'Dearle stars another one,'

'What?'

Netta made a cutting motion with her hand. 'Forget it. Just make sure you don't get hurt again and check in more frequently, okay?

Echo queried politely, 'To Bendrix?'

Exasperated Netta snapped, 'Yes, female, who do you think I am talking about?'

'At this stage of the conversation—'

Netta leaned into Echo a little and growled dangerously, 'Are you trying to annoy me?'

'Ahh no, but I see I am doing so without working too hard at it.' Echo grinned as she said, 'Imagine what I can do if I try.'

'Oh, my stars!'

Echo shrugged as she told her, 'Leaving now.'

Netta looked after her and muttered, 'I think I hate her. I need to apologize to Bendrix.'

Echo laughed quietly to herself as she made her slow way to medical and into Heather's office. Heather was sitting at her desk with her feet up on a footstool. 'You wanted to see me.'

Heather frowned but did not remove her feet from their perch. 'No… umm, do I?'

'So Netta told me.'

'Oh, the after-mission health check. Why did Avery not perform it?'

'She is all loved up with Mayton.'

Heather's face softened, 'Oh, how lovely.'

'If you say so. So, the exam?'

Heather dropped her feet to the floor and then pointed to the examination bed. 'Sit up there, please.'

Echo jumped onto the bed and waited while Heather grabbed her scanner. 'How are you feeling?'

'Everything seems to work okay and I don't have any residue effects from the bolts. So on the whole, I'm good.'

Heather nodded as she ran the scanner over her, then checked the reader. 'Everything says you are well. Have you visited Jarrod yet?'

'Ahh no, am I meant to?'

'Yes, it is mandatory in cases like yours.'

'Oh, I did not know that. Someone should write all this stuff down.'

Heather grinned. 'Someone has. It is in the mission manual.'

'There is a manual!?'

'Yes, and by your expression I can tell you have not read it.'

Echo shrugged as she admitted, 'I like vids.'

Heather murmured before she could help herself, 'So much like Peyton.'

'What?'

'Nothing, you are done.'

'Thanks, Heather. I'll get right on that other thing.'

'No matter, I assume they will notify you.'

'Oh, okay. Well, bye.' As she hastily exited the office, she was stopped again after walking only twenty steps. 'Negotiator Echo, just the person I need to see.'

'Seriously,' Echo muttered, then turned and smiled as she said. 'Greetings, Kail Jarrod. How are you?'

'Better now for finding you. So shall we go?'

'Umm, go where?'

'For you incident briefing.'

'What the hayda is that?'

Patiently, Jarrod explained, 'It is where you tell me how you are, what happened, and how you feel about it. Then I tell you, you are fit for duty and we are all happy.'

'But I am happy. Can I not just say we did that already?'

'I wish, but alas, no. Now come along.'

Echo grumpily whined as she fell into step with him, 'You know, you people are just nosy.'

'So, we have been told, nevertheless you will do as I wish.'

'Why?'

Jarrod looked down at the small female. 'Because you are liked and people want to be assured you are well and not just physically.'

That gave Echo pause, and she asked, 'Oh okay. Are you talking to everyone involved?'

'Yes.'

'Well, in that case, you should know Relic and Cleo are not

talking to each other.'

'Thank you.'

She gleefully told him, 'Any way I can help, just ask.'

She missed his sarcasm as he replied, 'I am sure you are full of information.'

The session was not as harrowing as Echo thought it would be, although she was still unsure what her feelings about her mother's death had to do with the attempt on her life but she didn't dwell on it. Her new motto was, do not dwell on things I cannot change. When she explained this to Jarrod, he had looked less than impressed. Still, he had only raised an eyebrow and told her he wanted to see her before she went on another mission.

THIRTY-SIX:

All things considered, Echo's first few days back home had been amusing and rewarding. She now sported new crimson nails and her hair was a dark blue color with hints of purple, reaching halfway down her back. She'd even had time to visit the new kits and spend some time with Matt and Shade rehearsing their dance, which she was happy to see they had mastered. Now she was looking forward to several days of quiet. She was even thinking of going on a vacation.

'Where are you going?'

Echo cursed silently when she heard Bendrix's question. She should have known the male would be skulking around her office.

Affecting a cheerful tone, she told him, 'Sorry, cannot stay and chat. I have to schedule interviews.'

Bendrix halted her departure by simply standing in front of her. He crossed his arms over his impressive chest as he asked, 'Is that not a task for your assistant?'

'Yeah, well, as to that.'

'Dear stars, do not say you fired another one.'

'She was noisy.'

'How so?'

'She talked incessantly.'

'That is part of an assistant's task.'

'I know, but she talked to me all the time.'

Bendrix frowned as his curiosity was aroused. 'What did she say?'

His piercing questions made Echo uncomfortable, prompting her to shrug in response. 'You know, stuff.'

'Like scheduling interviews and reading memos sent to your office from other departments, as in mine?'

Echo nodded, 'Yeah, stuff like that.'

Sighing heavily, he said, 'Echo, you need an assistant.'

'Says you.'

'Yes, as do Lady Brenda and Madam Peyton. Someone in your position needs an assistant.'

'I know, but I need someone with a military background who understands the Armee, not someone who cries when I get a little upset.'

Charis, coming from Chef Helen's office where she had been summoned to discuss Chef Enid, stopped and listened to the conversation between Bendrix and Echo. At first she thought Echo was being reprimanded, but quickly realized the Ambassador was trying to understand why Echo kept firing her assistants. As she listened, an idea came to her and she whispered, 'Oh now, let's see, could I... yeah, I could. So how do I go about making that happen? Oh yes, Lady Brenda.' She backtracked the way she had come and arrived, breathless and excited, at Brenda's office.

Meanwhile, Echo ended her conversation with Bendrix the same way she ended any conversation that annoyed her, she frowned and walked away. Bendrix was more amused than offended by her attitude, having witnessed it on several occasions. 'I am not finished with this conversation, Echo!'

She waved over her shoulder and growled, 'Whatever.'

An hour later, after a meal and having a swim in the new pool installed in a Hex on the edge of town, Echo was feeling in a better mood until she stood outside her office. 'Dayam it.' Sighing in resignation, she waved her hand over the entry pad and stepped inside, only to stop when she saw Charis sitting behind the assistant's desk. 'Umm, what are you doing?'

'Waiting for you.'

'Oh, excellent answer. Why?'

'I asked to step into the role of personal assistant to the Negotiator.'

'But that's me.'

'Yes, I know.'

Echo ran her fingers through her hair. 'You are a Warrior.'

'No, I was a Warrior. Now I am your personal assistant who will travel with you and do all those pesky things you need doing.'

Echo nodded, then walked over and held her hand out. Charis stood and took the proffered hand. 'Welcome. Have you squared it away with everyone?'

'Yes, Commander Hawk and Relic have released me, but I am to double as a guard so I still have to train with Relic and the others.'

'Oh, okay.' Releasing her hand, Echo stated, 'This will work.'

'Because I don't chatter?'

Echo grinned as she made for her office saying over her shoulder. 'That and you know Armee stuff, but mostly it is because I like you.'

'You do?'

Echo turned at the sound of surprise in Charis' voice. 'Yes, how can you not know that?'

'I guess after Kelara—'

'Let me stop you there. You and Ty did nothing wrong. It was what it was and we will make sure it does not happen again. In other words, we live and learn. Now, what do you know about scheduling appointments?'

'What is there not to know?'

'Come in and I will give you a list of people I need to see.' Once in Echo's office, she handed Charis a tablet. 'These are names of people who apparently, I have to see. Please schedule appointments for each of them over the next few days.'

'Will do.' Charis looked up from the tablet and smiled. 'Thank you, Echo.'

'None needed. I am thrilled to have you with me.'

However, over the next two days, her initial excitement waned. Her assistant turned out to be an efficiency expert and, worse, expected Echo to be one as well. In other words, she organized interviews at fifteen-minute intervals. Echo hardly had time to think before the next person she needed to talk to was sitting in her visitor's chair. Charis also did not take kindly to Echo escaping her office or making excuses to leave.

This morn had been no exception and when the door opened again after the last person had barely left the office, Echo barked, 'What now? Can I not get a min to myself?'

Helen kept her smile hidden and her tone mild as she entered the office. 'Perhaps if you are quick to answer my questions, you can have a min to yourself.'

Echo jumped to her feet as a blush stained her cheeks. 'I beg your pardon, Helen. It has been a busy morn.'

Helen took the visitor's seat as Echo retook hers. 'I hear a position with you is highly sought after.'

Echo brushed the hair off her face. 'I don't understand why, especially after what happened on the last mission.'

'You sound surprised.'

Echo enunciated each word. 'With… Me!'

Helen smiled. 'Echo, dearle, accept it as the compliment it is. They feel safe with you. And from what I hear, they like the way you find solutions without killing hordes of people.'

Echo rubbed her cheek as she told her, 'It is not always going to be that way and I tell them that.'

Curious, Helen asked, 'And what do they say?'

'They know and that is why they train or that is why I take Warriors with me. Variations of those themes.'

Helen shrugged. 'So there you are.'

'I guess.' Echo liked and admired Helen. She found her easy to talk to. Her no-nonsense attitude to life had spurred some very engaging conversations when they had first arrived on Maikonia. She wasn't really surprised to see her, not after she had dismissed Enid. What surprised her was how long it took for her to be here. 'So why are you here, Helen?'

'Chef Enid, you dismissed her, and I have been told by several people you did not get on with her.'

Echo decided to be as blunt as Helen usually was. 'No, I understand people, chefs included, have their opinions about food, what comprises a good diet but I eat meat. I love bacon.

My people eat meat. So to be denied meat for meals landed complaints on my desk which I passed onto Relic, who yelled a lot and mostly at me. So no, I do not wish her to return to the Intercessor.'

Helen raised her eyebrows at the straight-talking female. 'I see. Anything else?'

Now that she started airing her grievances, Echo told her about the biggest complaint she had. 'Dayam straight there is. Comfort food is just that, comfort food. If my people ask for a specific meal or… or cookies, then she should try to comply with their request. Not issue a ten min lecture on the benefits of abstaining from what she called junk food, don't yah think?'

Helen bypassed that question and asked one of her own. 'What exactly did Enid not cook in the way of comfort food?'

Echo's voice was sharp as she told her, 'Apple crumble dessert. Who cannot cook apple crumble? It's easy, even I can make it.'

Amused and slightly dismayed, Helen asked, 'What exactly did she do?'

Echo gripped her hands together on top of her desk as she explained. 'She told me apple pie was better for me and that raisins were good for my digestion. So that was why she put them in the pie. I don't like pie or raisins, which I explained to her.'

'You made her cry.'

'She gave me raisin pie, Helen. She was lucky that was all I did.'

'Echo, it was just apple pie.'

Echo sighed. 'I know some people like it but Helen, I like my apples two ways, raw or cooked in a crumble. Surely, it's not too much to ask that the chef cook a crumble.'

'No, dearle it isn't. I will assign someone else who is not averse to meat and can cook comfort food.'

'Thank you. It is important, you know, when we are away from home.'

Helen stood and agreed, 'I know, sweet girl. It helps to dull the ache of leaving home.'

'There will be times we are going to be away for luneras.' Echo shrugged as she also stood. 'So, there is that.'

Helen frowned as she looked at the young female. 'Yes, there is that.' As she turned to leave, Echo told her, 'I am sorry I made her cry.'

Helen laughed. 'Do not worry about it. She should never have said bacon wasn't a food group.'

'I know, right?'

'See you later, dearle.'

'If I am ever allowed out of here, maybe we can have tea.'

'Wonderful idea.' When she reached the door, she said. 'And dearle, try not to be so dramatic.'

Echo grinned as Helen whisked herself from the office, passing Charis who was walking in. 'I am sorry, Echo, she just walked right past me.'

'I understand. She is a force of nature. There is no stopping her.'

Charis blew a breath out in relief. 'You can say that again. Then, what did she say?'

'We will have a new chef. Someone who knows how to cook meat and comfort food.'

'Oh great, so your next appointment is here.'

'Of course they are.'

THIRTY-SEVEN:

Helen had a lot on her mind as she walked back to her kitchen. She had been confident that Enid could handle the traveling and the Wallace sisters, but she had no idea that Enid didn't know how to prepare meat. It seemed like Enid's aversion to meat had ruined everything. Now, Helen would have to pay Esther, who had bet that Enid wouldn't last. Helen hated losing a bet.

Walking into her kitchen, she found Clancy sitting at the table with several tablets open and a cup of tea at his elbow. The male was the same age as her Larson and just as handsome. He had a way of looking at a person with those green ringed eyes of his that made you think you were the only person in the room. He wore his hair short, not as he explained because he liked it that way, but because it was more hygienic. Clancy was not his original name, but one he adopted after watching his first western with Marlo. In addition to his new name, he had also taken on a western style of dress: jeans, checkered fleece shirts, leather jackets or long coats, and boots. She wouldn't be surprised if he had a cowboy hat, too. She loved his drawl, which had the power to turn her legs to jelly whenever he spoke.

She would never admit it to anyone, but the male was a better chef than herself or anyone she knew. He loved food, preparing and serving it, creating new dishes, cooking old ones, researching recipes from different worlds. He especially liked earth's recipes. Everything was a challenge to him. 'Greetings, Clancy.'

'Greetings, Helen, how are you this day?'

'I am well. I thought you were with Shodian Lujunn?'

Clancy closed his tablets and sighed. 'I was, but I have mastered Businnah. Shodian said he had nothing more to teach me.'

'Oh, I see. How long were you there?'

'Two days.'

Helen poured herself a cup of tea and took the seat opposite him 'So, what now?'

'I do not know. I have excelled at every class I have taken. I can make pastries, bread, candy, desserts, and have mastered every style of cooking on Maikonia. Even yours. I have filled five books with new recipes. I am done.'

Helen's eyes brightened as an idea came to her. 'Clancy, what do you wish to do?'

'Cook, I love cooking.'

Slowly, she smiled. 'Can you make a simple apple crumble?'

Instantly, his eyes sharpened. 'With or without cinnamon and raisins?'

'No raisins. Cinnamon, definitely.'

'Yes.'

She waved her hand towards her preparation area. 'Then do so.'

'Why?'

'I have a permanent position for you if you want it. But to get it, you have to pass the test.'

'And the crumble is the test?'

'Yes.'

'Very well.'

Seventeen and a half mins later, a delicious-looking apple crumble sat on the counter. Helen smiled in relief. 'Good. Jax, please comm Echo and tell her to come to my kitchen.'

'Immediately?'

'Yes, if she is available.'

'She will be relieved to have a reason to leave her office.'

Not long after, Helen asked Jax to summon Echo. Clancy and Helen heard running feet and then Echo burst into the room. 'Helen, I am here and please, please say it will be for the rest of the day.'

Exasperated, Helen shook her head. 'Echo, honestly!'

Echo fell into a chair and placed her head in her hands. 'Helen, it is horrific.'

'You are just holding interviews.'

'And that entails talking, so much talking.'

With a twinkle in her eyes, she said. 'I asked you here to introduce you to Clancy Turbine.'

Clancy smiled at the small female. 'Greetings, Lady Negotiator.'

'Oh, greetings. Have we met before?'

'No, but I know who you are. Ty is my friend.'

'Oh, nice to meet you Clancy. Please, call me Echo.'

'Thank you.'

Helen placed a bowl of crumble in front of her. 'I need you to try this.'

Echo looked at the food as if it was a snake. Suspiciously, she asked, 'Is it apple?'

'Yes.'

She sniffed it before asking, 'Does it have raisins?'

'I am not trying to kill you, Echo, although I see why it could happen. And no, there are no raisins.'

'Hey, I have to be careful. The last apple dessert was full of those little devlishes. I almost gagged.'

Helen muttered. 'How distressing, I assure this one has no raisins.'

'Alright, no need to get snippy.'

'Eat, now!'

Echo grinned at Helen's tone and could not mistake the humor in Clancy's eyes as she dug into the bowl of dessert. She would have licked the bowl clean, but Helen whipped it off her, leaving her holding her spoon. 'That was the best crumble I have ever eaten, and that includes my mom's.'

Helen replaced the empty bowl with a full one as she sat in her own chair and told her, 'Clancy made it.'

Echo eyed the quiet male and took another bite of crumble. She pointed her spoon at him and asked, 'What food group does bacon fall into?'

'For terrans, it has its own group.'

'Good answer. Can you make comfort food?'

'I cook for any occasion. Comfort is a class of its own.'

Without missing a beat, she asked. 'I need a chef to look after my people, and that includes comfort food. Would you be willing to work on my Battlecruiser? Actually, I should say for me as you will have to cook for me on worlds we are visiting.'

'What do you mean by work?'

'Run the diner on board Intercessor, and employ staff. You know, do your thing, but on a ship.'

Clancy cocked an eyebrow up as he looked at Helen, 'What do you think?'

'This position is made for you. Think of what you could discover. The food you could taste and learn to cook. You need to do this.'

He looked back at a grinning Echo and asked, 'I would be allowed to do this?'

'I would insist.'

He held his hand out for her to shake. 'Then yes, I would enjoy working for you.'

'Welcome to the family, Clancy.' She told Helen, 'He will have to go through the checks with medical and Relic.'

'Yes, I know, dearle. Off you go. I am sure you have places to be.'

'Yep, see you later, Clancy.'

'And you too, Echo.'

With a wave, she slipped out the door and they could hear her squealing, 'Yippeee!'

'Congratulations, Chef Clancy.'

Clancy chuckled, 'Thank you, Chef Helen. To think only a few hours ago I was worrying over what I could do with my life.'

'Sometimes if we are lucky, help will fall into our laps just when we need it. Although in saying that, the Wallace sisters are not easy.'

'So Ty tells me. Do not worry, I can handle this. Feeding people is my vocation and pleasure.'

'Alright, so let's get started. We have a lot to accomplish before the Intercessor is called out on another mission.'

THIRTY- EIGHT:

An hour later, Cleo arrived promptly at Echo's office and was greeted by Charis.

'Greetings, Cleo. How are you?'

'Greetings, Charis. I am well. You?'

'Okay.'

Cleo grinned as she asked her, 'Are you comfortable with your decision?' Cleo was one of the first people to know Charis had left the Armee for an office position. When she'd heard about it, she assumed it was because of the attack on Echo. But looking at her now, at the confident, relaxed way Charis held herself, she realized it had nothing to do with that.

Charis's smile was full as she replied, 'I am. I was never really comfortable with Armee life. This is what I did before I left earth.'

'So why join the Armee?'

Charis shrugged, 'I didn't know what else to do and everyone was joining up.'

Cleo chided her, 'Slim reasoning.'

Charis grimaced, 'Yeah, it was. But then again, it led me here.'

'And you are happy.'

'Yeah, I am. Cleo, my decision had nothing to do with Echo's attack. In fact, what I am doing is going to put me in front and center with her wherever she goes.'

'Yeah, I get that and I am pleased for you. You know I was going to ask you to join my unit.'

'You were?'

'Don't sound so surprised. You are a good Warrior, better than most terrans.'

Charis felt a warm glow as she ducked her head, 'Thanks, Cleo.'

Echo called out, 'If you have finished with the girly chitchat, Cleo, get in here.'

Cleo laughed as Charis shook her head and murmured, 'Armee life is looking good.'

Echo counted. 'Huh, should have thought of that before you kicked it. Now you are all mine,'

Sighing, Charis said, 'Go in, Cleo… please.'

Cleo laughed and with a wave to Charis, walked through into Echo office. She waved Cleo into a chair. 'So how have you been?'

'Good, settled back into home life easily enough.'

'It doesn't take much.'

'No, it doesn't.'

Echo casually asked, 'Any repercussions?'

'Not yet, but the hearing is for this afternoon, so we will see then.'

'Oh okay. Have you and Relic spoken?'

'Not yet.'

'I see.'

'What is it with the twenty questions?'

'It's a dayam interview. There are supposed to be questions or at least—' she pointed to the door between her and Charis, 'she told me that.'

'What do you want to ask me?'

'So bossy.'

'I'm a Commander. It is in the job description.'

'Did you like going out with me before the… you know what?'

'Ambush. It's okay, you can say the word.'

Echo frowned and mumbled, 'So touchy.'

Cleo grinned. 'To answer your question, yes, I enjoyed going with you as your Commander.'

'Want to do it again?'

'Is that your way of offering me a permanent position as your Warrior Commander?'

'Yep, that was it. Then what do you say?'

'I accept, if all goes well with the hearing, that is.'

'Whatever. So that is it. Welcome to the family.'

'Thanks.'

'Cleo, don't worry about the hearing. I think everything will turn out okay.'

'You have no idea if it will or not. What do you know about Armee hearings?'

'Not a thing, but I know people.'

'What does that mean?'

Echo shrugged. 'You are good at what you do and I like you.'

'Well then, what is there left to say?'

'Nothing, get out!'

As she stood up to leave, Cleo whined, 'Is this how it's going to be from now on?'

'Shut up and leave.'

Laughing, Cleo left as Charis entered. 'So, is she on board?'

'Yep.'

'What about today?'

'Today?'

Charis whined, 'Echo!'

Echo stretched as she assured her, 'It will be okay.'

'If you say so. By the way, there are no more interviews for today. You are free.'

'Yippee!'

THIRTY-NINE:

Ty sighed as he moved restlessly outside the office of the Amahka Elite. He hated interviews. They always made him think of things he could have done better and the things he wanted to do but never did.

'Enter Pilot Tyrrell.'

Taking a breath, Ty opened the door and entered the office to be confronted by not only the Amahka but Commander Kolin. He stood in front of Kardan's desk and came to attention.

'Amahka, Commander Kolin.'

'Pilot Hoya, welcome. Relax, this is an informal meeting.'

Relieved, Ty relaxed. 'Yes, Amahka.'

'I asked you here to determine if you wish to return to duty with the Negotiator.'

'Did she put in a request for me?'

'Yes, with one stipulation.'

Intrigued, Ty asked, 'Which was?'

'That you would be her personal pilot. It would mean you would have less flying time and would be removed from rotation, but it would be a permanent assignment. Is this acceptable?'

Without thinking too hard about what he was giving up, Ty agreed, 'I accept. When does my posting begin?'

Kardan smiled as he said, 'Immediately. I will inform Negotiator Echo, she will be relieved.'

'Did she think I would be unwilling to be her pilot?'

Kardan nodded, 'She was concerned because of recent developments you may have doubts.'

'It was not her fault she was ambushed. It was mine.'

'How so?'

Ty contended, 'I knew something was not right, the port felt

—'he struggled to put into words the feeling he'd had.

Jarrod asked from behind him, 'Wrong, as though the very air waited for something violent to happen?'

Turning quickly, Ty nodded. 'Yes, exactly, just like that.'

'You need training. I suspect you have a new ability coming to light.'

Ty was astounded, that possibility had never occurred to him, 'A new ability, like a Sene?'

'Similar to a Sene. We will have you tested. In your line of work, it could be an invaluable tool.' Jarrod looked at Kolin and said, 'I suspect that will answer your question.'

Ty looked at the Commander. 'What question?'

'How you shaved off thirteen mins from a twenty min flight.'

'Oh, that?'

'Yes, that,' Kolin stated. 'If you are finished with him, Amahka. I have some more questions for our pilot.'

'Yes, I am,' Kardan said to Ty. 'Congratulations on your promotion.'

'I am promoted?'

'Yes, to Commander.'

'Thank you, Amahka.'

'You deserve it for saving Echo's life and for your ability to pilot a shuttle like you did.'

Ty nodded, then left with Kolin. Kardan asked Jarrod, 'Will this new ability help him and keep Echo safe?'

'I suspect it will and more. We will discover what more he can do other than pilot a craft beyond its limits.'

'Good, keep me informed, please.'

'Of course.'

Once Jarrod left, Kardan comm'd Echo. 'You have your pilot.'

'Thank you, Kardan. What did you think of him?'

'He is an excellent pilot.'

'No, I mean as a person.'

'Ahh, he is well spoken.'

'And?'

Kardan blinked several times before admitting, 'I do not

know what else you want.'

'Never mind.'

'I feel I have disappointed you.'

'I am hanging up now.'

Confused, Kardan asked, 'Why are you hanging anywhere?'

Echo said before disconnecting, 'Kardan, you are hilarious.'

Kardan shook his head. 'I am at a loss as to why that was amusing. Jax, what is hanging up?'

'An expression terrans used to end a comm.'

'Strange that I have not heard it before.'

'I believe Echo recently watched an old vid from Earth.'

'I see, still it is disconcerting. Jax, do you find me hilarious?'

'No.'

'As I do not.'

'Do you wish to be hilarious?'

'I do not think so.'

'Perhaps it is worth investigating what is considered hilarious.'

'Perhaps.'

FORTY:

Cleo stood outside Conference room three. She had been ordered to appear at a hearing to explain her actions leading up to and after the attack on Echo. There was a small part of her that argued this could be her final day wearing her uniform. It was possible she could be demoted or retired. What, she asked herself for the hundredth time, would she do if she was not in the Armee?

'We are early.'

At the sound of Relic's voice, Cleo looked up from where she had been contemplating her feet. 'You think my feet are too big?'

Relic studied Cleo's feet in her Armee issued boots. 'Nah, they work with the rest of you.'

'Alright then. We okay?'

Relic came to rest next to her on the wall. 'Why shouldn't we be?'

'People talk.'

'Because they have nothing else to do. You have to remember people, other than present company and a few exceptions, are mostly idiots.'

'I will. So, you were ordered here, as well?'

'No, I came to back you up. No one should go into a hearing alone.'

'Seriously!?'

'Why do you sound so surprised?'

'You were really pissed with me, Relic.'

'Guilt is a bitchre.'

Cleo snorted, 'I know what you mean. I've been feeling a touch of that emotion a lot lately.'

Relic turned so her shoulder was against the wall and softly said, 'Something you should know about Echo. She never holds grudges against people she loves. Luckily, you and I fall into that category.'

Cleo turned so she was facing Relic. 'I say it again, you Wallace sisters are a strange breed.'

Relic grinned. 'That we are.'

'She offered me a permanent position on the Intercessor.'

'You mean with her?'

Cleo agreed, 'Yeah, I guess.'

'Did you accept?'

Smiling, Cleo asked, 'What do you think?'

'That, unlike my sister, you are not insane.'

'Is she, though?'

'Mostly, but once you realize that, you can deal with it.'

'She will get us killed.'

Relic laughed. 'Probably, but we will have fun until we die.'

'Well, there is that. Want to get a drink later?'

Relic sighed as she grimaced. 'Raincheck, I have this thing.'

'With Echo.'

'Yes.'

'Can I watch?'

'You and half the planet.'

'Why do you let her get away with stuff like this?'

'Did I not just tell you she is insane?'

'Oh yeah, I forgot.'

'See what she does?'

'Ahh, no.'

'Lulls you into a false sense of normal,' Relic slapped her fist into her hand, 'then wham!'

Cleo shook her head. 'Again, I say, you Wallace sisters are a strange breed.'

'Yep.' The door opened and Relic whispered, 'Here we go.'

They both straightened and waited while the door fully opened to reveal Marlo. When he saw Relic, he nodded. 'Good, now I do not have to send someone to find you.'

'Why would you do that, Commander?'

'So, you can answer a few questions?'

Relic looked at Cleo and shrugged. 'I see.'

Marlo muttered, 'Let us hope so. Please Commanders enter.'

'Sounds ominous,' murmured Cleo before she could stop herself.

Marlo grinned but said nothing as he closed the door behind both females. Larson stood next to two empty chairs at a large oblong table.

'Commanders, if you would sit here, please.'

They both sat and then waited as a door opened, admitting Hawk, Netta, and Jarrod. Behind them entered two large Prowlers that neither Cleo nor Relic knew. Suddenly, one Prowler stopped and turned to Hawk. He nodded twice, then the Prowler hurriedly left. Cleo watched the dusky pink female leave, her image imprinted on her mind.

When everyone had taken their seats, Hawk said, 'We will proceed without Bilaton. Jax will take notes. Present today are Commanders Hawk, Netta, Marlo and Larsen. Kail Jarrod and Prowler Daymon. Let us start.'

Larson read from a tablet. 'We are here to investigate the attack on Negotiator Echo Wallace. First, we will hear from Commander Cleo.'

She calmly reiterated, 'I do not know what more I can add. You have my report.'

Hawk requested, 'Explain what went wrong.'

Cleo nodded, 'After careful consideration, I have discovered there were several points of failure.'

'Which were?' asked Netta

'Lack of experience, no Prowlers, and complacency.'

Marlo nodded. 'Three excellent points. Can you elaborate on them, please?'

Cleo purposely relaxed her tense muscles. 'Of course. First, I believe if I had a unit or two of defenders, then the Raiders would not have remained hidden. Secondly, as for lack of experience, only more missions can help with that. The third one is directly my fault. After Governor Shaw was installed and the planet seemed settled, I stopped being as vigilant, therefore allowing the Assaen's to attack the Negotiator.'

Marlo asked, 'Are you saying if you had Defenders, you would have discovered the Assaens?'

Cleo had time to think about this since leaving Kelara. 'I do not know if the Defenders or Prowlers would have found them. I have come to believe they left the planet mins after the attack.'

'Without being seen?' asked Netta doubtfully.

Cleo nodded. 'Yes, either they were never there or they have some kind of tech that enables them to remain hidden.'

Relic asked, 'Like a shield of some kind?'

Cleo turned to her and nodded. 'Yes.'

Jarrod asked. 'What do you mean by not there at all?'

Cleo grimaced as she said, 'They shot a lot of bolts. Is it possible they did that by remote?'

Larson asked her, 'Did you find a remote-controlled device to support your theory?'

'No, but one could have been with the Raiders.'

Hawk sharply asked, 'I thought you killed or captured the Raiders?'

'I believe we did, Commander, but not one of the people caught or killed was an Assaen.'

Jarrod was the one to ask, 'How do you know this?'

'Commander Harm advised us they were not.'

Hawk studied Cleo for a few minutes without speaking, then he asked her. 'If we were to send you out on another mission, what guarantees do we have none of these problems will occur again?'

Cleo smiled before answering, 'None. The Defenders is only a matter of making a request which I am sure will be granted. More experience is, as I said, time and more missions. Complacency, well that one is for sure not going to happen again. But as for guarantees, I can only say I will do better, that is all.'

Larson asked, 'If we decide to demote you, would you remain a Warrior?'

Cleo winced, but bravely nodded. 'Yes, I love the Armee. Being demoted would hurt, but in time I would hope your trust would be renewed and I would again be able to Command.'

None of their expressions changed, so Cleo was unsure what they were thinking. She felt a sinking sensation roll through her and could almost see her command slipping away.

Hawk directed his next question to Relic. 'Commander Relic, you were made aware the Negotiator was going to the planet?'

'I was.'

'Can you explain why you sent only one guard with her?'

Relic's response was not long in coming. 'I would like to blame my decision to allow her to do so with only Captain Charis on inexperience, but I cannot. I was directly at fault. I, too, became complacent, but for me it was in the weapons used in this Universe. I prepared my guards for blasters and swords, knives even, but what I did not prepare them for, which was my mistake, were bolts. And because I was not prepared for them, neither were my people.'

Marlo asked, 'Are you saying you were not taught about bolts?'

'No, Commander, I am not saying that. We were all taught in weapons class about bolts. I am saying I dismissed them as an Assaen's weapon and as I believed there were no Assaens on the planet, I was unprepared.'

Larson asked, 'What have you learned from this?'

'Never underestimate your opponent to be sneaky and carry weapons you dismiss too lightly. I should have known better.'

Hawk asked the others, 'Does anyone have any more questions?'

Prowler Daymon said, *I have a question for Commander Cleo.*

'Yes, Daymon.'

Commander Cleo, if you were to keep your command, should we trust you to keep our people safe? And if so, why?

'I don't understand. None of my people were hurt.'

Daymon asked. *Why were you there at all, Commander?*

'We were there to secure the planet and to ensure the Negotiator remained alive and well.'

So, in both tasks, you were only partially successful.

'Yes, that is correct.'

Therefore, I ask again, what assurances do we have you can fulfill your missions?

'Oh, I see.' Cleo sighed, 'I cannot guarantee any of my people or myself will come home. No one can, except the Star Daughter. All I can do is learn from my mistakes so they do not happen again. That way I can protect my people and the Negotiator better.'

When no one else had any more questions, Hawk said, 'Commanders, you are dismissed. Thank you for your appearance here today.'

Both Cleo and Relic stood, bowed, and then left the room. When they were outside again, Cleo asked Relic, 'Did that go as you thought it would?'

'More or less. You?'

'The same.'

FORTY-ONE:

Matt looked up from his mid-day meal and into Echo's eyes as she sat down opposite him.

'I am sorry, did we have a meeting?'

'No, Relic is at the hearing.'

'I know.'

'So, she will go back to her place afterward.'

Confused by her statement, he nodded and said, 'I see.'

Echo scoffed at the lie. 'Do not lie, you see nothing.'

'Why are you annoyed?'

'Because tonight is the night, therefore today is the day.'

Matt stared at her for several long minutes before asking carefully, 'For what?'

Echo threw her hands in the air. 'Oh, my stars. Let me spell it out for you. You—' she stabbed their air between them with her finger, 'will go to my sister and make sweet love to her so that tonight we can show her all the wekens of practice you have indulged in.'

Matt's slow smile emerged as he nodded. 'I will do as you say.'

'Thank the stars.' Echo stood, then looked down at Shade. 'You should come with me.'

Why?

'Do you really want to be around him and her when they do the… you-know-what?'

Shade looked between his smiling bondmate and Echo. *Ahh, I think not.*

'Wise decision. Let's go.'

I will see you later, Bondmate.

Matt ran a hand down Shade's back in a caress, 'As I will you, Bondmate.'

Echo grinned as she wished him good luck. Matt stood as he

thanked her.

An hour later, he stood outside Relic's apartment. He knew she was inside; she was like a flame to his needar. He could scent her unique essence. It sang to him as nothing else in the Universe did. Matt knew Relic sensed he was there; he could almost feel her need for him. He placed his hand on the door and silently begged for permission to enter.

Relic paced her apartment. She knew Matt was on the other side of the door. She should never have listened to Echo when she talked to her this morn. 'Just talk to him Relic, how can it hurt? What do you have to lose? Relic grumbled as she paced her lounge again. 'I should have told her to butt out, but no… I just nod like an idiot and agree when she says I'll send him to you after the hearing.' She snorted with disgust. 'It's like I cannot organize my own life, dayam Echo.' She sighed as she stared desperately at the door to her apartment. 'And now here he is, standing outside my door.' Taking a deep breath in and holding it for a second, she released it as she smoothed down her dress, and bravely whispered, 'Come in.'

Pushing the door open, Matt's breath sawed in and out, as his chest filled with some unknown emotion. A vision of loveliness stood before him. Relic wore a long rose-colored gown that showed a lot of soft pale skin. He felt his body harden and the skin on his face tighten as emotions bombarded him. Then things got wild as his hearts started to beat together and he felt himself fade and reappear. He braced himself against the doorframe as he faded once more.

Shade called out to him. *Matt, what is happening?*

'Shade, I… I am having difficulty.'

I will come to you

Suddenly, Peyton was in both their minds. *'No Shade, stay where you are. I will help him.'*

Beloved what has happened to my bondmate.

'He is experiencing the onset of the mating heat.'

Oh… I see.

'Shade, he will be alright now.'

Thank you, Beloved

'Are you with someone?'

Yes, I am with Echo. We are watching vids.

'Oh, what are you watching?'

I am not sure, let me ask her.

Peyton grinned as she waited for him to return. *They are called musicals, and apparently you may not make light of them or her.*

'Musicals, no… no, I will tell no one.'

Beloved, do you lie?

'Oh, umm, maybe.'

Now more in control, Matt stood looking at his heart's desire… his Relic looked scared and yet beyond that emotion, hopeful and under both those feelings, he could sense waves of happiness. Before he thought about what he was going to say, words flowed from his mouth. 'I am bondmate to Shade and together we have what Peyton calls issues.'

'I know about your—' Relic grimaced as she said the word, 'issues.'

Matt sighed deeply. 'I see. I am sorry.'

Confused, Relic asked. 'For what?'

'For presuming you—'

Relic walked the five paces to her door, where he stood and grabbed a hold of his shirt.

'Get in here. I refuse to have this conversation with the entire world listening.'

Matt grinned as she released his shirt and he moved swiftly into her apartment, turning to watch as she slammed the door close and lean back against it. He said, 'I do not think—'

Relic cautioned, 'Stop there. That is what has gotten us both into trouble. We have thought too deeply about this.'

'Trouble?' Matt queried. 'How are we in trouble?'

Joy tingled throughout Relic's body. He was here in her apartment and talking to her, and she was talking to him. She opened her mouth to explain what she meant, but what came out was, 'I fell in love with you the moment I saw you.'

Matt's hearts pounded in his chest at her confession. He calmly asked, 'When was that?'

'Two days after we arrived home from the Capital, you were walking from the medical center with Jean. I thought you two were together.'

'Ahh, I see. This is why you never approached me even when you must have discovered I was unattached.'

'No, that wasn't the reason.'

Matt moved closer as he asked, 'Why?'

'I was frightened. I was not in good shape then, still underweight, still uncertain of what my life was to be, if we were really safe.'

Sighing, he said, 'I could have helped you with those fears and shown you what life was like on Maikonia.'

'I know.' By now she was looking up into his impossibly handsome face with his startling black eyes. 'I wanted to so much. Echo said I should but I could not.'

Matt reached out and brushed his fingers down her cheek as he moved even closer to her. 'Why?'

Relic swallowed and huskily admitted, 'I thought you would reject me.'

'Reject you!?'

'Yes. You are handsome. There is not a female I know who doesn't want you. Males respect and admire you. Peyton adores you, as do her sisters. I felt I could not compete with any of that. I am just me, Relic Wallace.' She shrugged and mumbled, 'And you are you.'

He wound a curl of her hair around his finger as she breathed in his scent, causing her to sway toward him. His voice was low and thrummed through her body as if she was a guitar string.

'I have spent my life waiting for you, wanting you. Not long ago, I asked Sedeen if there was any hope that someone would love me.'

'What did he say?'

'He assured me there was.'

'Love always finds a way.'

'Who said that?'

Relic smiled as she murmured, 'Echo. She believes in love.'

'Do you?'

'Oh yes, every day.'

'I love you, Relic. You make my hearts beat.'

Relic smiled as she wound her arms around his neck. 'Then all that is left is for you to show me what you have been taught in those sex ed classes you all took.'

As he scooped her into his arms, he boasted, 'I excelled in my class.'

Relic laughed. 'I am sure you did.'

FORTY-TWO:

At the same time Relic was being swept off her feet by Matt, Cleo returned to her apartment to be confronted by the large Prowler who had left the conference room. Cleo looked her over, then greeted her. 'Greetings.'

Greetings, Commander.

'Is there something you want?'

My name is Bilaton.

Cleo frowned. 'I am sorry I do not recognize that language.'

Cleo could feel the shame that washed over the Prowler and her heart hurt for her. *My pride named me. It means dirty one.*

All expression was wiped from Cleo's face, although she could do nothing about the burning rage in her eyes. Her voice when she spoke was quiet as she told the Prowler. 'You should change your name. Where I come from, we would call your coloring sunset pink. It is beautiful just as you are.'

Bilaton ducked her head. *I would like to change my name. I feel unwashed every time someone uses it.*

'I understand. Would you like to come in?'

Yes, I would like that. She looked up at Cleo. *Do you know who I am?*

'I have a good idea, but I also know you will not say the vow until you have a name that makes you proud.'

Bilaton was relieved. *This is so.*

'Well then, let's get you a name so we can get bonded.'

As Bilaton moved aside so Cleo could unlock her door, Cleo said, 'You do realize they may demote me and we will not be going out on any missions.'

I do not think that will happen.

'Why is that?'

You are an excellent Commander. Inexperience does not

disqualify you. Not willing to learn from your mistakes is the only thing that will disqualify you.

'Well, that is not me. I always learn and make it right.'

Which is why you will not be demoted. As they entered Cleo's apartment, Bilaton said from behind her. *Beloved does not agree with demotions.*

Cleo grinned. 'Good to know. Now let's get down to the business of finding you a suitable name.'

Yes, breathed a relieved Bilaton.

Minutes later, they were no closer to a name that either of them liked when Cleo's comp pinged to alert her to an incoming transmission.

'Greetings, Cleo.'

'Greeting, Echo. How are you?'

'I was going to ask you the same. How was your hearing?'

'I think it went okay. I am waiting to hear what they decide.'

'Are you worried?'

'Of course I am. Is Relic?'

Echo shrugged, 'Who knows? She is with Matt, so you know.'

Cleo grinned. 'So, she finally admitted he is the one?'

Echo grinned as well. 'Yep.' She looked past Cleo and spied Bilaton. 'Who is your new friend?'

Cleo turned slightly as Bilaton moved closer to the screen. 'I am sorry, dearle,' to Echo she said, 'this is my bondmate or almost bondmate.'

Echo frowned. 'What do you mean, almost? Either she is or she isn't.'

'We are trying to find a name she likes. Her old name Bilaton means dirty one.'

Echo's frown intensified as she told Bilaton. 'I bet your pride gave you that name because they could not see the gem you are. Oh, that is a good name.'

Cleo asked, 'What… Gem?'

'No, look up Opals. They are a precious stone from earth.'

'Why?' asked a suspicious Cleo. Exasperated, Echo ordered. 'Just look them up, then you will understand.'

'If you say so.'

After Echo disconnected, Cleo looked at Bilaton. 'What do you think?'

She is the Negotiator?

'Yes.'

And your friend?

'I believe so.'

Then let us look at this precious stone.

Together they searched the comp for information and pictures on Opals and were stunned by what they found. 'Wow, they are spectacular!'

Most beautiful, and the Negotiator thinks I look like an Opal.

Cleo murmured, 'That she did, and she was right. Oh, look at this one. It has your coloring.' She pointed to a stone that was light pink with patches of lavender.

The lavender is the same color as my eyes. It is beautiful.

'Yes, so what do you think? Do you like the name Opal?'

Bilaton stared at the picture of the beautiful stone for several minutes. Cleo did not rush her. This was a big decision for the Prowler.

Finally, she said, *I am unsure.*

'Of what?' Cleo asked as she ran her hand down Bilaton's back.

Am I worthy of choosing such an arresting name?

'Most definitely, you are worthy. In fact, the name really does not do you justice. I think you are far more beautiful than the name implies.'

Then I will be proud to be named Opal. She looked at Cleo and recited the words that would bind them together. *I am Opal; I am for you.*

Cleo smiled as she took Opal's face in her hands and whispered, 'I am Cleo Gibson; I am for you.'

FORTY-THREE:

As the second sun set on Maikonia, Kardan entered Peyton's office to find her tinkering with a bot. 'Are you allowed to be doing that?'

Peyton glared at the driver in her hand. 'Yes, Kolin, gave it to me.'

'Should I ask why?'

Peyton looked at him and smiled, 'Probably to keep me from the complex.'

Kardan sat in her visitor's chair as he asked. 'My heart, you have not threatened to go to the complex again?'

'Threatened?'

'Yes.'

Scowling at the accusation, she asked him, 'Why are you here?'

'Avoidance is a sign I am correct.'

'Or it is a sign that I do not want to discuss this.'

'Because it will make you wrong?'

'Kardan!'

'Whining is another sign.'

'Alright, alright. I may have suggested it was time for me to visit the complex.'

'Peyton, why?'

'I was bored. You were gone. It seemed like a good idea at the time.' Her expression was contrite as she said, 'I know it was wrong.'

'Good. Now I am here to give you the results of the hearing.' He passed her the tablet he had been carrying.

She read the report and nodded several times. 'So, they have been cleared of any wrongdoing?'

'I did not read that.'

'It's what it said.'

'No, what it said was they were both found to be deficient in areas of their training which will be rectified.'

'So cleared.'

Kardan sighed before agreeing with her.

'Yes, but with reservations.'

'Yes, I read that. They will be relieved.'

Kardan smiled as he assured her, 'Not as much as Echo, but yes, I am sure they will be. There were also other recommendations.'

'Do I need to know what they were?'

'No, they are about military procedures.'

Peyton aid thoughtfully, 'So Echo has her people.'

'It would appear so, and a few extras.'

Peyton hummed to herself for a few minutes before saying, 'I do wonder what Matt and Relic will do now they are mated.'

'Yes, I have thought about that myself. What do you think? Will they stay home or travel?'

Peyton shook her head. 'It is hard to say.'

'What would you prefer?'

'They travel with Echo. I think Matt would be invaluable to her.'

'I agree. It will be interesting to see which way it goes.'

Peyton agreed, then asked, 'Have you heard from Reeve?'

'Just a message to say they have arrived at the Capital and are to see several people Darby had found to question.'

'Good, and what does Rata report?'

'Nothing yet. She has sent out several members of her family to search for information, but so far no one knows why Echo was targeted.'

'Okay.'

'Do you want to tell Echo?'

Peyton thought about it for a moment. 'No, let's keep this official, send it through military channels.'

'In other words, you wish me to speak to her?'

Smiling sweetly, she nodded. 'Yep.'

Penny came in. She had a blush to her cheeks as she breathlessly told them, 'It is happening.'

Peyton yelped, 'What is happening? Not the babies. I am not ready.'

Penny grumbled, 'No, not the babies. You know not everything is about you being ready.'

'Stop lying. It so is.'

'No, it isn't.'

Kardan sighed as he stood up and brought their attention to him. 'Ladies, please. Penny, what is happening?'

'Echo and Relic.'

Peyton jumped from her seat. 'Why didn't you say so, Penny? We have to go come on, Kardan.'

'Where are we going?'

'To the thing.'

'What is a thing?'

Penny and Peyton both stared at him. Peyton asked, 'How do you not know what the thing is?'

He shrugged. 'I guess it is because I am a male.'

Penny's eyes twinkled as she said, 'He's right, Peyton.'

'Well, yeah, but he's an Elite… The Elite!'

'Still a male,' murmured Kardan.

'Regardless, you need to come with us and witness something you are unlikely to experience again.'

'I have—'

'Nothing!' Peyton grabbed his hand and dragged him from her office after Penny.

Kardan was amused to see people streaming from offices with excited expressions. 'This must be truly amazing.'

Peyton agreed, 'It is, just wait.'

She dragged him into a transfer circle, and before he knew it, they had arrived at the indoor training arena, which looked completely different. The usual training mats were covered by a large oval platform, surrounded by rows of tiered seats rising from the floor. Peyton led him to a seat about halfway up, where Netta and Bendrix were already sitting Hawk and Karen arrived with Wolf and Jarrod.

Peyton asked Jarrod, 'Where is Trina?'

'She is with the babes. She will watch on screen.'

'Are your parents coming?'

'They would not miss this.'

'Good.'

'What is this?' asked Kardan again.

'You'll see.' Was all Peyton would say and as he looked around at the others, he saw they were not going to tell him either. Sighing, he resisted the urge to check the time; he had several things that required his attention, but it seemed they would have to wait.

Penny sat next to Kerol as Heather and Harm arrived and made their way to the seats in front of Kardan and Peyton. Then the Prowlers arrived, led by Briark and Leiark. Soon, almost every seat in the arena was filled.

Netta told Peyton, 'Darby is going to be pissed she missed this.'

'So will Reeve,' murmured Wolf.

Peyton agreed, then assured them, 'We will send them the vid.'

Netta gasped as the two sisters entered the arena from opposite sides, 'Oh, my stars, they are dressed for battle.'

'What are they wearing?' asked Helen, who was seated with Larson, Marlo, and Brenda. Esther sat behind them with Jorge and Amelia.

Netta replied. 'Leather vests and pants,'

Dillion growled. 'It is not practical for battle. They would die with all their soft skin exposed.'

Peyton grinned as she explained, 'Dillion, sweetie, it is like a ceremonial battle. They are not really fighting; it is more like a dance.'

'I do not understand. They are bearing arms.'

Which they were. Both sisters carried swords. Coraan and Melody slipped into their seats just as the lights went out, leaving the stage in darkness. Hawk explained to Dillion. 'This, is a special kind of dance, one the Wallace sisters have only ever performed once before.'

Surprised he knew this, Peyton asked, 'How do you know?'

Hawk smiled as he told her, 'Echo told me when I granted permission for them to dance.'

Netta asked, 'When was that?'

'This morn.'

Confused, Karen asked, 'So this is what, then?'

He told her, 'This dance symbolizes the end of one stage of the sister's lives and the start of another.'

Karen squinted into the darkness, trying to see either of the sisters as she said, 'But they are not leaving each other.'

Peyton shrugged. 'It is symbolic and the last time they danced like this was when their mother died and they left earth.'

Heather, sitting in front of them, murmured, 'Oh my stars, how sad.'

'For us perhaps, for them, a release,' stated Jarrod.

Heather asked, 'Where is Matt?'

Harm said, 'He will be here.'

Peyton asked Harm, 'What are you going to do about him, now he is with Relic?'

'I have assigned Matt and a unit to Echo permanently.'

Kardan asked before Peyton could, 'Is he pleased with that?'

'It was his idea, and it was a good one. Echo said having Mayton and his unit was invaluable. Cleo said they would have lost Warriors without his Intel.'

Netta agreed, 'It's a good idea, Echo will need someone who is knowledgeable in the ways of the Universe and its people.'

They all nodded silently as they watched two transfer circles flare to life, admitting Mayton and Avery, Charis and Cleo with Opal. Melody smiled when she saw Cleo and Opal. She turned to Peyton and told her, 'Bilaton chose a new name when she bonded with Cleo.'

Peyton, watching the couple find seats, asked, 'What did she decide on?'

'Opal.'

'Such a pretty name.'

Melody agreed. 'It is. Apparently, it was Echo's suggestion.'

Peyton nodded. 'It sounds like something she would say. She has a heart of gold.'

'Well hidden,' muttered Netta.

Peyton tapped Heather's shoulder and told her, 'We are going to have to assign another Healer to the Intercessor.'

Heather half turned to face her and smirked as she said, 'By we, you mean me.'

'Well, I cannot do it unless you want me to?'

'No, no. I have it under control.'

'So, who have you picked?'

Melody asked, 'Why are you replacing Avery?'

Harm explained, 'Mayton is needed elsewhere and Avery is his mate, so—'

'Oh, got it.'

Peyton asked Heather again, 'So, who have you chosen?'

'I have several candidates I am looking at.'

'So, no one!'

'Shut up.'

'So rude.'

FORTY- FOUR:

Just before the lights went off, Relic asked Echo, 'Are you ready?'

'Are you?'

'Yeah.'

Echo frowned as she whispered, 'You don't sound it.'

'I am… it's just that—'

'Just what?'

Relic whispered, 'Echo, we didn't get the markings.'

'What markings?'

Relic blew a breath out, trying to quench her frustration and worry. 'You know… after we… you know!'

Echo hissed, 'Oh, my stars, just say sex.'

'Shut up.'

Echo laughed softly. 'So, no tatts, big deal.'

'It is a big deal. Everyone gets them. Peyton said so.' Relic sounded depressed as she whispered, 'You think it could be a sign?'

Bemused, Echo asked, 'A sign of what?'

'That we shouldn't be together.'

Echo sighed. 'No, but if you are worried, go see Peyton after this and talk to her.'

'Oh, good idea, we'll do that. Thanks, Echo.'

'What are sisters for? Now let's get this show on the road. And Relic—'

'Yeah?'

'Don't miss, sister of mine.'

Relic grinned at the warning. 'You, too. Remember, I am a mated female now. I need all my bits in one piece.'

'Eww, I cannot believe you just said that.'

Relic flipped her sword in her hand as she muttered, 'You are just jealous.'

Echo declined to answer as she hurried to her place on the stage. Gradually, soft spotlights penetrated the darkness and illuminated the stage, revealing the crossed swords resting on the floor in front of the two sisters as the lights settled on them. When the lights expanded, both Echo and Relic were in position, one hand on their hips, the other curved in the air. As the music started to play, both sisters began to dance, stepping lightly over the swords, never touching a blade. Hopping from one foot to the other in a dance handed down from generation after generation.

Kardan quietly told the others seated with him, 'This is called the highland dance or the highland fling. A traditional dance passed down through the family.'

Hawk asked as he admired the sisters' foot work, 'How do you know this?'

'I have studied where the sister's ancestors came from. This dance came up in my research, although I have never seen it performed.'

The music softened and slowed, and before anyone knew what was to happen, both sisters swooped down and picked up their swords. Then, as the tempo of the music changed, so did the dance. Both sisters twirled and stepped around the stage, always ending in front of each other, their swords poised to strike. Several times, the audience gasped, expecting blood to be spilled as the swords came within a hair's breadth of a sister's face or neck.

Admiration filled Heather's voice as she murmured. 'So much control, they must have practiced for hours.'

'Or are just that good?' Netta stated, she would admit later to Bendrix she was impressed with the sisters' skill.

Melody asked Netta, 'Could you do that?'

Netta slowly nodded, 'The sword work, yes, the dancing, hayda no!' which caused everyone to laugh softly.

As the beat of the music gradually increased, so did the speed of the dancers. Soon, it was almost impossible to follow the movement of the blades, let alone the sisters, as they moved across the stage. Then, as the music and dancers reached what had to be the crescendo, everything stopped. The sudden silence and stillness were almost painful after so much sound and fury. Relic and Echo stood absolutely still as they faced each other with only inches separating them. Their swords crossed and held at each other's throats.

Brenda clutched her chest as she murmured. 'Dearle stars, I never saw that coming,'

Helen let go the breath she had been holding. 'Exhilarating.'

Esther's only comment was, 'That's one word for it.'

'What the Hayda?' Heather whispered as a bead of blood pebbled on each blade,

Kardan once more explained. 'I believe the cuts on either side of their necks represent the cutting of the family ties.'

Melody stated, 'Yep, they are just that good.'

Harm whispered, 'You are right, to do so and not sever the arteries is masterful blade work. I am impressed.'

Peyton grimaced. 'Seems a bit extreme. A simple goodbye would do it.'

Netta murmured as the music began again, 'You are not a Wallace.'

Slowly, the sisters stepped away from each other, and in a coordinated move they lowered their swords, placing them on the floor. When the music changed to a soft, slow rhythm, the sisters began to dance. Their movements were a study in grace and fluidity, each step and the position of their arms conveying a tale of sorrow and loneliness, happiness and love, for those who had the ability to decipher it. As they moved across the stage, their bodies almost touching, everyone realized their movements mirrored each other's exactly.

Frowning, Netta asked, 'Is that a shadow behind Relic?'

Melody replied, 'It can't be. Echo doesn't have one.'

'So, what is it?'

'Shhh!' growled Peyton.

Netta and Melody grinned, but remained silent.

The sisters glided over the entire stage in a choreographed dance, their movements combined with the music sighing through the arena, making the females in the audience think of long romantic nights with their mates.

Just as everyone began to wonder what more was going to happen if anything, half the stage lights went dark. Leaving Relic dancing by herself. As if it had been scripted, the shadow behind Relic detached itself from her and Matt appeared. Relic spun around when she felt someone at her back and discovered Matt stepping in perfect time with her. 'Oh!' she breathed as he took her hands in his and they began a dance that spoke of love and a future for the two of them. Then another shadow detached itself from Matt, and Shade mirrored his bondmate's steps.

Echo watched from the darkness as Matt and Shade led Relic through the dance she had taught them, with one final glance at the couple she let herself out of the arena, whispering softly. 'I did it mom, her heart is safe now.'

Matt kept his eyes on Relic's shocked ones as he whispered, 'I believe we have surprised you.'

Laughing joyfully, she replied, 'You have indeed.'

'Good, it bodes well for our future.'

Smiling, Matt once more led her through a set of intricate steps he had taken wekens to learn, neither one noticing the blue and purple bands appearing around their wrists or Shade once more disappearing. The dance ended with a kiss as the lights slowly faded to darkness.

Penny gushed, 'Oh my Stars, that was so romantic.'

When the lights came back on, they saw the stage was empty and people began to leave.

Peyton asked Kardan, 'What did you think?'

He took her hand in his and helped her stand. 'I think we should have a place for dancing. It looks like something couples would enjoy. I know I would.'

Smiling, Peyton agreed. 'I will ask the Ladies' club what they think.'

'Thank you for not allowing me to miss this. It was

extraordinary but I cannot help thinking Echo is now alone.'

'Yeah, but not completely.'

He sighed, 'I hope not.'

As they made their way to the circle, Peyton asked, 'You really like her?'

'I like them both, but Echo's burdens are heavier than Relics will ever be and she has someone to share them with now while Echo does not and her burdens will only become heavier as time moves on.'

'So, we need to care for her more!'

He stated, before stepping into the circle. 'You are most wise.'

Peyton told him with a grin, 'I get that a lot.'

'So boastful!' he told her as he stepped from the circle.

'So rude.'

FORTY-FIVE:

Echo sat curled up in her chair on her balcony watching the first moon rise. She sighed as she sipped her coffee.

'Are you upset?'

Echo clenched her hand around her mug at Peyton's sudden appearance. 'Come in, Peyton, please, don't let a door stop you.'

Delighted at the sarcasm, Peyton sat in the vacant seat opposite Echo. 'So, are you?'

'No, at least no more than I thought I would be. Up until we left earth, we lived apart most of the time. We only got together occasionally.'

Peyton nodded. 'He will be good to her.'

'Oh, I know and now he has Shade she will never feel alone. I could not give her that feeling of togetherness that she needs to make her feel whole.'

'Will the scars disappear?'

Each of the sisters was now carrying another silver scar on their necks. Echo traced the old scar and shook her head. 'No, the first ones didn't disappear even when I went for a spin in the regen. I think they are a gift from the Star Child.'

Peyton relaxed back in her chair. 'I imagine they believe you are entitled to a memory.'

Echo agreed. 'That is what they are, memories of good times. I am happy they remain.'

'Do you still want her as your Commander?'

'Goes without saying.'

'Have you talked to Kardan yet?'

'Yes, I am happy they were both cleared.'

'You do know someone is hunting you?'

Echo sipped her drink before acknowledging that. 'I know. But forewarned is forearmed and I will not allow myself to be ambushed again, nor will I allow my people to be hurt.' She looked over at Peyton and could almost hear Relic demanding she use her manners. 'Would you like something to drink?'

'Yes, please. Water.' As Echo rose to get her a drink, Peyton thought about what she'd said. When she returned and handed her a glass of cold water, she asked, 'Do you have any idea who it could be?'

Echo grinned as she asked her in return, 'What would make you think I would know?'

Peyton scoffed. 'Please, I know you have been researching world's that are associated with Assaens.'

'They are really targeting you and Kardan.'

Peyton shrugged. 'We know, but you are the one they are aiming for. So, any thoughts?'

Echo laughed and gave in. 'I have narrowed it down to five worlds who may believe they have cause to target you through me.'

'Such as?'

'Earth for one.'

Peyton frowned as she sipped her drink, then said thoughtfully. 'Feasible, but distance makes it unlikely. Who else?'

Echo silently agreed with her. She had placed Earth on her short list but more for form's sake rather than she believed they would actually hire Assaens. 'There is Uthrio. You have to admit they have cause. They are not happy about the sanctions and they have Assaens.'

'True, but I think it is also unlikely. Klune sent them a clear message that we would not tolerate any retaliation for the sanctions. But still worth investigating. Who else?'

'Fractions within Patamogol.'

Peyton shook her head. 'No, definitely not. I see how you could come to that conclusion, but the Emperor or his brothers would know before us. They have a firm hand on their jewel houses, which are the only ones who could afford Assaens.' Peyton caught Echo's cynical expression and sighed. 'Yeah, I know, we cannot discount anyone. So a word to the Emperor's brother would not go amiss.'

'Thank you. It's best Lord Klune says to cover all the obvious ones first.'

'Yeah… Yeah. Who do you have next?'

'That would be Odehrema.'

'Ahh, now that is more than likely. They are not at all happy with me and I can see them hiring Assaens to target you thinking your death would embarrass me and put doubt into the minds of the other world leaders.'

Echo agreed. 'That was my thinking, and I thought perhaps the Raiders for the same reason.'

'Yeah, we thought about them, but we think they were used as much as the Assaens were.'

'What do you mean?'

'We think both Raiders and Assaens were not on the world when you arrived but arrived later, after you had taken over.'

Echo felt her way through that idea as she murmured almost to herself. 'Because how else did they hide from Cleo's Warriors or Mayton's? And no one knew we were arriving.' Echo nodded her head. 'So yeah, I see that.'

Peyton nodded when she came to the same conclusion, she and Command had come to. 'That was our thinking.'

Echo sipped her coffee then said, 'It makes sense. Although how did they get past the Intercessor? Surely the Commander would have seen the ships arriving?'

'Klune believes someone has developed a new stealth technology.'

'Oh dayam, how do we combat that?'

Peyton grinned. 'Now that is why we have spies and inventors.'

'Oh yeah. So basically, we have to be vigilant and not allow our security to become lax.'

Peyton stood as she said, 'That about says it all. Keep thinking about who else could want you dead. You are good at it.'

Echo grinned 'I sort of have to, really. It is my skin, after all.'

Peyton grimaced, 'Well, there is that.' Before she left, Peyton asked her, 'Are you lonely, Echo?'

'Not in the sense you mean, but sometimes I get a little down.'

'Is there anything I can do to help?'

'Thank you, no, it is something I deal with. I probably drive people crazy while I'm doing it, but there you go. We all cannot be Relic.'

'Or Darby,' moaned Peyton.

'Oh stars, you have one, too?'

Peyton laughed before saying, 'I do like you.'

'Thanks. For a Star Daughter, you are not too bad yourself.'

'Talk soon, Negotiator.'

'I am sure we will,' Echo said as Peyton disappeared in a column of flame. 'That is so cool.'

EPILOGUE:

Echo leaned against the bar as Cleo grumbled about noisy places and Charis sipped her drink while she scanned the room.

Echo shook her head and said again, 'I cannot believe you've never been here before.'

Cleo grinned as she stared at Charis, who asked her, 'Are you talking to me?'

'No, her.' Echo pointed at Cleo, who shrugged as she looked around the bar.

'Not really my thing. So Charis, do you come here often?'

'No, not often. But it is a great place to meet people.'

Echo grinned as she teasingly said, 'Yeah, Cleo, you can meet people here… like the opposite gender kind of people.'

Cleo lowered her glass and stared hard at Echo before saying, 'Seriously, fixing your sister's life wasn't enough? Now you have to start on mine.'

'Yep, or hers.' Smiling, she pointed at a grinning Charis.

Before Cleo could retort, Ranarra Daygoniss walked in and captured her attention. She watched as several females and males dragged him off to a table by the far wall. Cleo's jaw tightened as a female she did not know placed her hand on Ranarra's arm and leaned into him. Much to Echo's delight, she heard Cleo hiss when the female threw her head back and laughed, then stretched up and kissed his cheek.

'Oh my, someone has it bad for a certain draygon.'

'Shut up, Echo.'

'Cleo, is Ranarra your mate?'

'Again, I say shut up.'

'Why?' asked Charis. 'He is cute.'

'You shut up as well. I am not talking about him.'

'You should talk to him, Cleo,' Charis said before slurping the rest of her drink.

Cleo adamantly shook her head. 'Not gonna happen.'

Charis pouted. 'But he is so cute. I would date him, all those muscles and wings. Oh, my stars, those wings… mmm!'

Cleo asked with a glint in her eye that should have warned Charis, 'What did you say?'

'I said—'

'Nothing, she said nothing,' interrupted Echo, as she moved discreetly in front of Charis. 'You cannot kill her, Cleo, just because you are all jammed up about the delectable Draygon.'

'Yeah, listen to our boss,' chimed in Charis.

Echo took Charis' glass off her saying, 'And that is enough drinking for you tonight.'

Charis whined but allowed her to take her drink. Cleo glanced over and saw another female stroking a hand down Ranarra's wing and hurriedly looked back into Echo's knowing eyes. 'Time to go.'

'Yeah, sure,' agreed Echo.

The following morning, Matt found a message on his comp from Kardan.

Commander Kato, I wish Ranarra Daygoniss to be included in your unit to serve Negotiator Echo Wallace.

TRANSLATIONS:

Adee = Living malleable unknown substance

Amahka = Mate to Star Daughter

Ambassador = Ambassador

Armee = Army

Anult woue = Attack Dog

Artar = Veterinarian

Assaen = Assassin

Basterads = Bastards

Bitchre = Bitch

Businnah = Asian style food. Boo- sinn- ahh

Cabu = Cow

Cassuam = Engine

Castque = Out Cast

Chanderoh = Imposter/ clone

Chinsee = Goatee beard

Circlet = Made to work as a whore

Comparium = Engine

Coverup = Make-up

Data drive = Flash drive

Data Flick = Data Chip

Darma = Trader word for mother

Dayam = Damn

Dearle = Dear

Desoul = Demon

Devlish = Devil

Domard = (Doe-mard) Protect and guardianship of people, worlds, planets, living organisms

Empirer = Palace

Falears = Faders

Feelons = Felons

Funta = Joke
Furin = Fuck
Furiner = Fucker
Genea = Geneticist
Gesovo = Vow
Gravatron = Force or traction
Greeting = Hello
Guardiod = Adopted
Guardio = Adopted parent or Guardian
Guardioan = Adopting/adoption
Hayda = Hell/Hades
Healers = Doctors/ surgeons
Hiesie = Conmen
Hikaran = Chess, four levels played in 3D
Hoay = Gay Male
Hutell= Motel/Hotel
Impoef = Pretender
Kailee = Mystic Queen
Kail = Mystic King
Kilto = Mile
Lalorla = Lawyer (Lalora)
Laroro =Accountant (La-roe)
Layra = liar
Lituiumin = Type of alloy (lit-tui-umin)
Lunera = Month
Luslian = Precious metal
Masters = Mind Healers
Matar = Mother
Mecon = Senator
Min = Minute
Mins = Minutes
Mystics = All of the mystical people
Narto = Narcotics
Needar = Being/ Spirit/ Soul.
Nutoro = Idiot
Olesho = Asshole

Omperea = (Om-pear-ah) Mystic word for great mother
Parta = Trader word for Uncle
Plasium = Platinum
Poho = Ghost
Primer = Level of technology advancement, low med, high
Priounty = Reward/Bounty
Prowler = Turquall
Raccinor = 'Race- in- orr' Motorbikes
Rie = RYE Soul fire. Inner spirit. Well of power
Rogu= Stew
Roments = Pig like animal with eight legs
Santinue = Drug used for Turquall
Sargann = Guards
Savgell = Animal
Scallut = Female whore
Scallup = To whore oneself
Scaloup = Male whore
Schrouse = Special heavy water
Scup = Smug
Sene = Seer
Sevna = Mystic Priestess, Avana
Shaymar = Finder/Searcher
Snikes = Snake crossed with a lizard, Venomous
Somnea = Leather
Somneline = Mammoth animal used for leather
Soytou = Cow carcass
Shosole = Steroid Drug
Suula = Soul bond
Swarm = group of Draygon fighters
Sybilla = Mystic- discovers and trains special abilities
Taje = Jerk
Terran = Human
Tetamoant = Sampler of food
Thsieon = Thieves
Tivna = Priestess,Melody.
Tocho = Matchmaker (Toeco)

Tournat = Sword duel
Tornays = Tournament
Tuarillians = Original Turquall
Tuap = Torp- Shit
Turquall = Large cat
Unta = Trader word for Aunt
Urnu = Guard, nanny
Upio = Deer like animal with six legs
Valard = Concierge
Varsteram = Ability to read emotions
Walkways = Escalators
Wetera = Material
Weken = Week
Whiskay = Whiskey
Woian = Gay female
Woue = Dog
Yenta = Year

Watch for further adventures of the Negotiator...

OTHER BOOKS BY L.M. LACEE

Daughter of Ethos: Prequel Book 0.5
Daughter Of Ethos: Unknown Universe Book 1
Daughter Of Ethos: Destination Home Book 2
Daughter Of Ethos: Price of Power Book 3
Daughter Of Ethos: Divine Justice Book 4
Daughter Of Ethos: Deadly Betrayal Book 5
Daughter Of Ethos: Crystal City Book 6
Daughter Of Ethos: The Ascension Book 7

Check LMLacee.com for more.

www.ingramcontent.com/pod-product-compliance
Lightning Source LLC
Chambersburg PA
CBHW051049250726
48656CB00001B/211